YOU CAN'T

The Story of an Amish Deacon's Son Who
Left the Fold and Became a Doctor

Albert Miller MD & Liz Miller

YOU CAN'T DO THAT!

Printed by Zilarellim
Printed in the United States of America
Available via www.zilarellim.com and other
Cover and Graphic Design: Grazielle Portella

First Printing Edition, 2022
ISBN 979-8-9859468-5-7

This book is dedicated to:

My parents, who instilled in me a firm belief in God and a strong work ethic.

My siblings and their children, if you read this it is my hope you understand that my absence in your life for all those years was not my choice.

My children, Elizabeth, Michael, Kristina, Sara, and stepchildren Todd, Elizabeth, and my wife Patricia thanks for each of your support, love, and for making my life complete.

Nothing in the world can take the place of persistence. Talent will not: nothing is more common than unsuccessful men with talent. Genius will not: unrewarded genius is almost a proverb. Education will not: the world is full of educated failures. Persistence and determination alone are omnipotent.

Calvin Coolidge

CONTENTS

APPENDIXES

THE AMISH

ABOUT THE AUTHORS

A DAUGHTER'S FOREWORD

Growing up as an Amish child, my father went on to become a doctor despite never attending high school. I spent years asking my father to share his story in book form, but he never quite got around to doing it. He finally agreed to let me write his memoirs for him.

The project was complicated by the distance between us: me living in Sao Paulo, Brazil, and he in Dothan, Alabama. A glass of wine or two kept the stories flowing during several father-daughter vacations in Brazil. Struggling to make headway across an ocean and in different time zones, we worked diligently over the past four years to finally put the spoken tales I had heard in my youth on paper.

Although my dad reads a lot, I can sometimes watch the typing ... message lingers under his name on Whatsapp for 10 minutes before I finally receive two lines of text. Typing was never in his skill set; he was accustomed to having a secretary type what he dictated. If we had waited for my dad to type this story, you would likely not be reading these words now. Taking a page from his private practice back in the 1990s, I modernized the dictating technology. He sent me voice messages of notes, which I transcribed and compiled into this book.

In addition, I read the most recent academic sociological research on Amish communities and solicited input from my father's still-practicing Amish brothers and sisters, sometimes via a phone call from a hunting blind. Together, with the help of friends and family in both the English and Amish communities, we organized the story of his journey into the book you hold. It is not a complete biography of my father's life, but rather a look at specific moments where he sought answers to the fundamental question of whether to remain in the Amish community and the challenges and division his choices created.

I like to think that my dad and I are a lot alike. Maybe that comes from the fact that I can identify in so many ways with his story, despite never having been Amish. Both of us made lives we love in cultures that were not our first environment, stubbornly venturing into the unknown even as those closest to us constantly warned us of the dangers of the "other." We both adapted and even learned to thrive in our new homes, learning things we did not know from new friends and laughing at the mistakes we made on the way. Switching between languages has become second nature, yet at times I think we both feel a pang in our hearts when we can't quite remember the word we wanted to say in our first language. Perhaps that's because we have stepped so far away from our roots that our cultural baseline has shifted.

I love that my dad just goes out and does things. He sets a goal and doesn't ponder it, but does it. This is one of the traits I like to think that I picked up from him: the idea of setting a goal and doing all in your power to make it happen. It might not happen the moment you want it to, but sooner or later you get it accomplished. The doers, not just the talkers, as I like to think of it.

Time and experiences have shown that those who speak more than one language and know more than one culture (though not exclusively these people) tend to be more empathetic and understanding. It is no surprise to me that both my dad as a doctor and I as a teacher ended up in fields that require tireless compassion, empathy, and responsiveness to others' needs. My father is by no means perfect, but I admire him deeply for his courage in confronting the many challenges he faced and his tireless persistence in working to overcome them. I'd like to think I inherited some of these traits from him, including perhaps his skill for surprise and timing. Never would I have imagined halfway through writing this book that I would question who my biological father is, but both my dad and I love a good story.

It is our hope that his experiences will help others who face challenges and struggles in their life—and who doesn't?—whether small or large, feel empowered and reach for their goals. No matter how many times they hear "You can't do that!"

INTRODUCTION

America is a land of dreams and hopes, and also of secrets. Other countries see only snippets of American culture, so they often assume cheerleaders and football stars rule the land, and anyone can be anything. Yet those who have lived in America know the truth: Each person makes America their own dream, with their own ideas, and no one person can ever experience all the intricacies of America. The stories hidden behind every hill and the diversity behind every doorway are astounding, and truly understanding America's contrasts and rich complexity would take many lifetimes. In a country where technology leaps toward the stars in Silicon Valley, there are other areas where time stands relatively still.

Time is a funny thing. You hold it like the last snow of the spring, but the tighter you grasp it, the more it slips through your fingers, and you can never get it back. Most of us think we have all the time in the world, but the minutes and hours and days melt away, shifting and changing from solid to liquid to gas until suddenly they're gone. So too the Amish culture has been shifting and changing throughout time, often in unexpected ways.

The Amish church was first formed by Jakob Ammon in Europe in 1693, with practitioners immigrating to the United States between the 1730s and the 1850s to escape religious persecution[1]. Since their arrival in the US, the

---

[1] Kraybill, Donald B., et al. *The Amish. Baltimore*, MD: Johns Hopkins University Press, 2013.

Amish have long fascinated other Americans. Their unique lifestyle—the ways they intertwine culture and religion—often clashes with the lifestyle of those around them.

Across the United States, the Amish are recognized as a symbol of traditional values and closeness to nature, yet most people do not recognize the glue that binds the Amish together. The Amish believe that living simply is living closer to God, and they do this through a strong sense of community in which all things are done for the greater good of the community and God.

Because the Amish have not changed much in their traditional dress, to outsiders it may look as though they have stood still in time. But throughout history, Amish communities have adapted, just in different ways than their neighbors, the "other" Americans, or English as the Amish call the non-Amish.

During the almost two decades that I lived and farmed with my datt (dad), little changed in the life of the community[2]. We milked cows by hand and kept the milk cans in a trough of running spring water to keep it cool. In the summertime, it was too warm to keep the milk cool over the weekend so we had to use the milk right away or it would spoil. Because the Amish religion forbids buying or selling anything on Sunday, we could not have our milk picked up on Sunday. On Saturday evenings we ran the milk through a separator, a device that separates the cream from the whey, keeping the cream for my mother's cooking. The whey we fed to the pigs.

---

[2] For more details on typical Amish life and my own experiences in the community, see "The Amish" section at the end of the book.

Due to governmental regulations, the Amish are no longer allowed to process and sell their milk the old-fashioned way. Temperature control regulations and other requirements from the FDA forced the Amish to adopt automatic milker systems and keep milk cooled in refrigerators run on propane or natural gas. Electricity to run these refrigerators may also come from solar panels, gas generators, or battery packs.

Six decades ago, few people, let alone the Amish, imagined harnessing energy from the sun. Solar panels were unheard of in my youth. We used kerosene or gas lanterns in the house and Coleman gas lanterns, similar to those for camping, in the barn. Nowadays, some farms have light bulbs run on the same energy source as the milker, and my brother uses solar panels to keep his chicken coops warm. Many farmers use battery packs to operate electric lights, though they are still not allowed to use electricity off the grid. And much more light is available with larger propane lamps or natural gas lamps instead of kerosene lanterns in the house.

When I was growing up, hay balers were not allowed; they were considered too modern. Now hay balers—pulled by horses—are no longer banned.

Modernization gradually changes all of our lives. Just as my fascination with cars must have seemed strange to my father all those years ago, now I too am awed by the technological advances as I record voice messages to my daughter that she transcribes halfway around the world.

The Amish are not exempt from the push of technology; they simply resist change, and it happens at a much slower pace for them than the rest of the world. Yet over time even they are forced to give in as changes are pushed upon them by society. The most striking change I've seen is the rapid growth of the Amish community and the scarcity of farmland.

When I was growing up it was rare for an Amish family not to earn their living off the land. However, Amish communities grew rapidly, and now the land is too scarce a commodity for the Amish to live solely off their farming. Many Amish now run their own businesses—furniture manufacturing, engine repair, carpentry, masonry, leatherwork, handicrafts, and other similar occupations. Some Amish men work in lumber mills or in factory-type jobs like pallet makers in facilities operated by an English friend or neighbor.

Thus modernity creeps into all our lives. It eats away at tradition, so slowly you don't notice it. The Amish world has gone from kerosene lanterns that hardly provided enough light to read by to large floor-based natural-gas lanterns. Likewise, a society that has long lived hidden behind their simple clothes and quaint ideas is now interacting more and more with the English world around them. Little changes have exposed a world formerly left in the shadows, and I am perhaps the embodiment of those changes.

Time is slowly killing us all. Not in literal death, as we tend to think, but in the death of cultures and lifestyles we once held dear. I imagine that the Amish known to my grandchildren will look quite different from the Amish of my youth. The lifestyle will have eroded and changed so gradually that only in looking back over decades can we see the changes. Time is a slippery thief.

So before the days slip from my grasp, let me take you back

to my youth. A time not so long ago, but different since now it is hidden under the trappings of modern society. A time when the Old Order Amish lived and thrived in their traditional ways. A time when it was acceptable to shun a wayward son. That is where my journey began.

PART 1
THE AMISH WAY

WHOOPING COUGH

Wheeze, pant, cough, cough, gasp. It is so hard to breathe. My lungs keep coughing the air back up. The cough hurts so much, that I just want to rest for a while and not try to breathe. *Cough, wheeze, wheeze, gulp.*

Memm (Mom) and *Datt* (Dad) have taken me somewhere new. It's not like the farm; everything's cold and white. *Cough, cough, gasp.* People crowd around the crib where they put me. A kind old man in a white coat leans over and straps a mask over my face. The air in the mask feels cold and fresh. It smells sticky and sweet, and it's a little easier to breathe. *Gulp, gulp.* The coughing subsides and my chest doesn't feel so heavy. I lie down and close my eyes. I'm so tired from trying to breathe and not cough! Soon I curl up and fall asleep.

The human mind has the ability to store memories more clearly than what we can consciously bring to light. But as children, we are often told stories over and over again until we can't tell where memory starts or stops and imagination takes over. I know that when I was only 10 or 11 months old, I spent almost three months in the hospital—a story I have heard more times than I can count. I don't believe I have any real memories of this time, although I can picture it vividly.

When I arrived at the hospital with whooping cough, I was whisked off to the pediatric ward. The doctor sat my parents down for a serious talk.

"Your son has whooping cough, a highly contagious bacterial infection. We are giving him antibiotics and oxygen. However, we are not sure how effective the antibiotics will be since the disease has already progressed significantly, and he is struggling to breathe. He will need to stay here in the hospital and we will do everything we can to ensure he is comfortable and well attended to, but you must understand that considering his age and the progression of the disease, we aren't sure how long he can hang on. You should prepare yourselves for the worst and take this time to say your goodbyes."

My parents nodded in stoic silence.

"We have a social worker and a chaplain available if you would like to talk to somebody," said the doctor, his voice heavy with concern.

One of the hallmarks of the Amish teaching is that as God's children we are all forgiven. As much pain as my possible death might have caused my family, they firmly believed that my soul was saved and I would go to heaven, and this belief gave them some peace.

"Thank you, we have our own people for support," my father said gruffly, then he and my mother began to pray. The Amish stick together to support and help each other in times of difficulty, whether illness, accidents, fires, or natural disasters. My father would have viewed any help coming from non-Amish clergy as worse than useless, a potential portal to evil.

This was the first of many times the doctors told my parents to prepare for my impending death. While not usually life-threatening in older children or adults, whooping cough, also called the 100-day cough, can be highly problematic for children younger than one. Young children do not cough so much as simply stop breathing, and antibiotics are only effective if the disease is treated early on.

Lucky for me I was always stubborn, even at this young age.

Despite repeated predictions that I would not survive the night, I continued to struggle and fight for air.

My memory of this time is glimpses of light and images that I've always considered more guided imagination than true memories. Perhaps it was simply an innate curiosity and desire to help others that later inspired me to become a doctor. Yet maybe it was the image of the kind man who gave me that first life-saving lungful of oxygen. I often wonder if my encounter with hospitals at such a young age created the passion for helping others through difficult times that led me to spend the greater part of my life in those hospitals.

FIRST QUESTIONS

The Amish religion consists of many sects, all of which consider themselves Christians. The two sects near my home were the Old Order Amish and the New Order Amish. While both groups strove to be separate from the world and live a pure life that was pleasing to God, New Order Amish taught that Jesus died for our sins and believed people were saved by grace. They encouraged faith education through Sunday school and Bible studies.

In contrast, Old Order Amish emphasized adherence to the doctrine of the church, believing members earned entrance to heaven by obeying the rules. Old Order Amish followed a strict code of ethics, enforced rigid restrictions on technology, and maintained the traditional austere dress style.

While the Amish are not exempt from military drafts, they can opt to serve as conscientious objectors, which includes service not on the front line but on farm camps or in hospitals to fulfill their obligation. When my datt completed his required service during World War II, he married my memm and bought a farm in Coshocton County, Ohio, where I lived and worked for the first 18 years of my life. The farm was in the Old Order Amish church district known as the Clark district, which crossed from Holmes County into Coshocton County. We were one of only about two Amish families in Coshocton County.

Life on the farm started early enough for us to see every sunrise.

"*Boova es ischt tzite fah uh schtay.*" (Boys, it's time to get up.) "Mose, Eli, Jecky, Albat," Datt called up the stairs at 5:30 AM. He went out to feed the cows as we pulled on our clothes. Milking the cows was always the first of our morning chores. While Jacob led the cows into their milking stations, I tugged on my rubber boots and grabbed a milk pail and a milking stool.

It usually took four or five of us to milk all 14 or so cows. If five of us were milking, we each only had three cows to milk, which would take 30–45 minutes. But when only two people were available for milking, it could take well over an hour.

Like most Amish boys, I started learning chores between the ages of six and eight by helping one of my siblings or Datt. By the time I was nine I had my own cows to milk.

Every morning I sat down next to Nellie. It took me 10 or 15 minutes to empty her udder before I moved to the next cow, Maddy, and on down the row until the last cow was milked.

When I finished milking, it was time to feed the horses, and finally the pigs. We all helped each other until these tasks were done.

By 6:30 AM the animals were taken care of. Only then would we head in for our own first meal of the day. As we sat around the breakfast table, we knocked the last of the sleep out of our eyes with coffee soup: a steaming bowl of coffee and warm milk poured over bread or saltine crackers floating over a hidden treasure of bananas and sugar. It was the perfect way to wake up.

Some days Memm made scrambled or over-easy eggs, or perhaps French toast with sausage. We almost always had homemade bread with jellies canned from the berries that grew on our farm. Whatever Memm made is what we ate; it wasn't made to order, and we ate a lot. Working through the morning until lunch every day meant that we got to eat our fill every mealtime.

When I was growing up, we were surrounded by English neighbors. At age four I wasn't much help on the farm, but I loved going out in the fields with my datt. I sat under a tree or climbed as high as I dared, guarding Datt's bottle of water against imagined marauders and watching as he made his rounds plowing the fields. Slowly the two-horse team dragged the single-furrow plow back and forth to carve grooves in the soil for planting the season's crops.

When I got tired of sitting, I pretended to plow my own little corner of the field. I searched out the perfect tools: a stone, narrow and sharp to cut the deep grooves of the plow; some jagged stones for the disc that tilled and smoothed the soil, ready for planting; and finally, a rounded stone to serve as my planter. Once I gathered the tools, I marked out my own little plot of a few square feet. In my mind, it was an enormous field and required diligent use of my imaginary equipment.

Sometimes after I finished tilling and planting, I looked across our farm to the hill that belonged to our English neighbor, Ralph Kaser. He used a tractor that pulled four plows at the same time. Mr. Kaser's work went so much faster than Datt's! He could finish in a quarter of the time it took us. His tractor didn't need to stop and rest from the hot sun like our horses. All the extra time it took my father to plow each field gave me plenty of time to ponder about our life compared to that of our English neighbors.

Why don't we use a plow like Ralph's? We could plow and plant more land faster.

When one of us gets sick, or one of our animals, we always go to Ralph's to call for a doctor. If it's wrong to have a phone, shouldn't it be wrong to use someone else's phone?

We can't own a car, but we can ride in his car or in an Amish taxi to go to the doctor. If it's wrong to have a car, shouldn't it be wrong to ride in a car?

Why don't we just get our own phone? Our own car? Why can't we plow faster like Ralph?

The Amish don't baptize babies the way many churches do. They believe that joining the Amish church must be a conscious, deliberate choice, and children are expected to make that commitment as an adult. Growing up, though, I still had to follow all the Amish rules. The whys I asked were never answered, and in fact, my datt frowned whenever I asked them.

The Amish want to make sure changes, especially technological advances, don't affect their relationship with God and their community. Two all-day church services, which non-members couldn't attend, were held each spring and fall. On those days the church reviewed and sometimes modified its doctrines: decisions about farming equipment, technology, transportation methods, or dress, and any amendments to rules. The first service was known as the *Ordnung* (*de adniks gehme*), or doctrine church. Each new rule was decided on as a community, led by the bishop with input from the preachers and deacon. I remember when the church changed its policy on hay balers and milkers, eliminating the prohibitions on such equipment so Amish farmers could comply with government regulations and remain active in the US agricultural community.

Members of the church who didn't follow doctrine would be excommunicated, meaning they couldn't take communion (*de Grose Gehme*) or vote on new doctrines until they had made things right. Reasons for ex-communication ranged from having rubber-rimmed tires on your buggy instead of the required metal ones to allowing your Rumspringa child to keep a car on your property. Essentially, members who didn't follow the rules were banned from important church events until they rectified their sins.

Since as a child I wasn't a part of these decisions, it seemed to me that the rules were not well explained. When I asked questions about why we did things the way we did, I always got the same response: "*Sel iz ischt vie es ischt.*" (That is just the way it is.) "Do not question the will of God. Your grandpa would turn over in his grave to hear you asking that."

What Grandpa Miller would think always seemed a moot point to me. He had died before I was 10 years old, and the idea that my questions would make him roll over in his grave always puzzled me.

No one ever explained things or answered my questions. Everyone simply attempted to shut down my curiosity. Instead of trying to help me understand, the community shamed me into listening and doing what I was told, and not questioning the status quo.

As I got older and started real work in the fields, other questions flooded my mind. In the summer heat, Ralph sat on his tractor, shirtless, but I was never allowed to take my shirt off or even just wear my undershirt. This disparity did not make sense to me.

If God can see and know what is in my heart, then He must see the T-shirt I'm wearing under my shirt. So why can't I just take my shirt off and wear my T-shirt when it's so hot?

At the age of 12 or 13, I came to the conclusion that I would never get the answers I sought about the Amish ways. There was no one defining moment that marked this decision, just an ongoing inability to get any of my questions answered.

And they were always swirling around in my head. I knew I wouldn't be able to rest until I found the answers.

Why can't we have a tractor?

Why can we ride in a car but can't own one?

Why can we use electricity or a telephone from someone else when we are sick or the animals need care, but can't have our own?

Why does our church have rules about the number of buttons on our clothes?

What is the difference between the over-shirt and the undershirt if God sees them both?

I decided that when I was old enough, I would try to find answers on my own. Even then I realized that might mean looking for answers outside our community. With so many unanswered questions and so many whys in my head, I chose not to join the church when I came of age, so I never learned some aspects of the church rules and the rituals.

The search for knowledge led me down a path very different from that of my brothers and sisters, even though two of my brothers, Eli and Jacob, also considered leaving. I watched how the community talked them out of their plans, and knew that my departure would be different. Oftentimes our greatest adventures start not with some life-altering event, but with a mere question.

A DAUGHTER'S QUESTIONS

Some of these same questions I would go on to ask later. Like everyday life, there are a lot of double standards. It didn't make a lot of sense to me that the Amish could ride in cars but not drive them. Just like it didn't make a lot of sense to me that Jesus said to treat others like you would want to be treated, yet some people in Christian churches did all in their power to exclude 'the others' – the LGTBQ+, the downtrodden, the divorced, and those who really needed the most help.

Where was the line drawn for what was necessary for farm production and what wasn't? When did people decide to "reinterpret" Christianity to make it fit their own desires versus holding to the core teachings of the Bible?

Why was it OK for my one uncle to use solar power but my other one didn't? Why was it OK for some pastors to marry and others not, and why for many could a woman never be a pastor?

If the Amish can accept one uncle using solar power, why can't they accept my dad? Why were some sins considered more deadly than others?

Amish relatives called my father for medical advice, but almost nothing else, for many decades. Did he feel used?

Some questions you ask from generation to generation and there's never a 'right' answer or one that really satisfies that itch to understand. There is always the taste of hypocrisy in each and every generation. The explanations from hypocrites seem watered down, weak — not well thought out. Later they say, it could have or should have been different — but why wasn't it?

It is the "why" that hounds us from generation to generation.

SCHOOL

I attended Keene Public Elementary school until sixth grade when I was transferred to a one-room Amish schoolhouse. Most Amish churches have their own parochial school system, but because we lived at the edge of our community, no school was within walking distance. Though we were the only Amish in the school, we were treated well.

At home and in our community the language spoken

was Pennsylvania Dutch, a German dialect. Every day the yellow school bus stopped by our house to pick us up for the 20- to 30-minute ride with our English neighbors. We never felt different, despite the contrast in our dress, but the language barrier was shocking at first.

My older brothers and sisters had been going to Keene for a few years when I started there. I had picked up a few words from them, but the first grade was when I truly started to learn English. Other than occasional interactions with the milkman or the doctor, I had never needed to speak it. Even our dentist spoke Pennsylvania Dutch. It wasn't until I started school that I even cared about learning English.

Like any new first grader, I was apprehensive at first, but I made friends quickly. Ms. Karr was my first-grade teacher when I started school at age seven in 1960. The milkman's wife, Mrs. Parkhill, was my second-grade teacher.

By third grade with Mrs. Overholt, my English fluency was lagging behind the other students in my class. To help me catch up, I was placed in speech class with Mrs. Lamison. Even though I wasn't the only one in it, speech class made me feel a little strange. Because the local schools were too small to require a full-time person, the speech therapist traveled from school to school throughout our rural community.

On the days she was at my school, she called each of us in to work with her for half an hour on our difficulties. She made me practice particular sounds over and over again, telling me where to put my tongue as I read different sentences aloud. I struggled with pronunciation issues, especially the "r," "d," and "th" sounds. *Mother, brother, father* came out as "moter, broter, fater." Pennsylvania Dutch doesn't have the "th" sound, so learning how to pronounce it correctly was tricky.

At first, the sessions were fun as I learned to make the sounds and pronounce the words correctly. Before long, though, I got bored practicing the same sounds and sentences over and over again. But I learned fast and had them down in a few months. Mrs. Lamison noted on my report cards that I was "a hard worker who was very cooperative and learned easily."

The other students at the school came from rural backgrounds as well, so we had a lot in common. That didn't mean I always felt like I fit in.

It wasn't just the language struggles. When playing ball on the playground or talking about everyday things, my classmates treated me the same as everyone else, but my friends knew things I didn't know about. In conversations on popular culture like the latest episode of *The Beverly Hillbillies*, I felt left out.

More than my different clothing and odd habits, such exclusion made me feel separate. Other students didn't make fun of us, but we never fully integrated into the school environment. We weren't allowed to play instruments or be on any sports teams except to play ball at recess. We didn't participate in any after-school events. Our focus for school was good grades, and we all got those. I don't think I ever got a C except in handwriting.

A DAUGHTER'S SCHOOLING

I think my dad and his siblings got lucky at school. I remember when it was just my family and one other at our Catholic elementary school tarred with the word divorce like a scarlet letter we wore in shame to school, even though we hadn't been the ones to choose that 'divorce' thing. We were excluded from events, and friends could only hang out with us depending on whose home we were at. The other home (usually my dad's place) was considered evil or tainted by the word – divorce.

While my father bravely went to first and second grade and made friends, I found my letter of shame something to hide behind. I stayed hidden in my books at that time not really understanding what divorce meant at that age or why people acted like they could catch it from my siblings and me.

Could you catch a divorce? If so, perhaps I gave it to the rest of my class. By the time I was in 5th grade nearly half the classes' parents were divorced. By the time I was in high school it was rare that friends' parents were still in their first marriage.

Until my dad started sharing this story I forgot I also was pulled out for speech classes with my brother when we were kids. My brother had a bit of a lisp but for the life of me, I can't remember why I had to go see Mrs. Rose the speech therapist. It was just one year or so, in 4th or 5th grade. It is funny how something so impactful for my father barely registers in my memory despite having a similar experience.

Grades were always our top priority in school and came easily to me like my father. The only Bs in elementary school I ever got were in handwriting. Now I like to explain that by saying I inherited my father's handwriting since he's a doctor - people smile and laugh knowing it's almost impossible to read what doctors write out for patients. Perhaps poor handwriting just runs in the family.

Like my father, I always felt left out not having much knowledge about TV either. Growing up my mom rarely let us watch it. We had two hours of TV time a week. The four of us kids had to agree on what to watch and could only use our time on the weekend. My mother insisted we spend our spare time reading books instead, so I never knew the shows my classmates watched on the weekdays. I couldn't participate in those conversations and add that to my parents' divorce - it was almost impossible to make a 'cool' impression.

Looking back on it though I'm really glad I wasn't allowed to watch much TV as a kid. I think my love of reading adventures has led me to some of my greatest real-life explorations. The tidbits I picked up from books proved far more useful than TV topics as an adult. Plus books are a comfort, a safe haven from the woes of the world, to always fall back into if you just have a bit of light to read by. Who knows, perhaps if I had watched more TV I wouldn't have been inspired to be writing these memoirs.

Still, kids make mistakes. Mistakes that I look back on with embarrassment, even many years later when I taught the same lessons to my own kids. Wanting to fit in often leads children to go against their better instincts, and Amish kids are no different in that respect.

Money wasn't something we saw much of as Amish kids. I remember being proud when I had saved a whole 13 cents in my piggy bank. The other rural farm boys I knew often had a few cents to buy candy, and sometimes they shared it with me since I hardly ever had any money on me. Near Keene Elementary was a little store that students could walk to and buy bubble gum and candy. The bubble gum was one cent apiece.

One day my buddy didn't have money, but he had an idea.

"Let's just take the bubble gum. We can just grab two pieces. They'll never notice, plus we buy it from them all the time, so it won't matter."

"I don't know. Doesn't that count as stealing?" I asked.

"It's only stealing if you get caught, and we won't get caught. I'll distract them and you grab two pieces. No one will know. You're Amish. They'll never suspect you."

"That still doesn't make it right."

"C'mon, I buy you candy all the time. Do it this once for me."

Against my better judgment, I shrugged and went along with the plan. He did, after all, buy me candy often. I should do something for him in return, right?

When we walked into the store my palms were already sweaty. My friend went to talk to the owners while I looked at the gum.

The squares of bubblegum sat in a bowl, hidden from the clerk's view. I had reached my hand in hundreds of times before, but this time was different. Ignoring the 1 CENT PER PIECE sign, I grabbed two pieces and stuck them in my pocket. I walked out as casually as I could, my buddy following close behind.

During the whole walk back to school, I felt a shadow looming over me. When we got to school, I took the gum out and popped one in my mouth. I felt so guilty my stomach hurt. The gum tasted bland - as if the flavor had been sucked out of it. I kept looking over my shoulder, convinced that the police would arrive any minute. I was certain the store owners had seen me, not to mention the trouble I would be in with my datt.

"I won't do that again. I'm not risking going to jail for gum," I worked up the courage to say, my voice far more confident than I felt.

My friend just nodded.

A DAUGHTER'S CONFESSION

It's peculiar some of the first times we do something we know is wrong. We have this rush to do something thrilling, but oftentimes the thrill falls a bit flat. I still remember in 8th grade when my friend Alison and I stole a beer from my parents' fridge. We had heard so much about beer that we wanted to know what it tasted like. We snuck out and went for a walk. Cracked open the can. It fizzled and smelled awful.

"You take the first sip," she said.

"No, you can, I replied." She crinkled up her nose in disgust as she did.

I followed, and "Wow! Why does everyone want to drink this stuff? It tastes awful! You want more?"

"No, it's really gross. What should we do with it?"

I dumped it out into the grass, after just two sips and we put the can in the neighbor's trashcan convinced we had accomplished a great theft and gotten away with it!

A day later my dad sat me down.

"Elizabeth, I'm not going to be mad if you did, but I want you to be honest with me. Did you take a beer from the fridge?"

My 8th-grade self caved quickly, "How did you know? We didn't even really drink it, Dad, it tasted awful. I swear we dumped it all out, we just tried it."

Looking back I think my dad was trying to hide a smile.

"Well, there is an odd number of beers in the fridge, and Pat and I always drink together."

Of course, I thought mentally, we should have thought of that and taken two. Though then we would have had to throw out two cans!

"Next time if you would like to try some alcohol, please ask. I don't mind letting you taste some of mine, but I don't want you sneaking around."

Unfortunately, that wouldn't be my last time sneaking around, but it did teach me that telling the truth is important. Sometimes we learn more by telling the truth than by lying.

Ralph Kaser's kids, who lived on the next farm, rode the bus and went to school with us. We knew them reasonably well since Mr. Kaser took most of our livestock to the market with his truck. We didn't play much with his kids; we only associated and played with our Amish neighbors. However, since we all went to the same school, one summer the Kaser family invited us to vacation Bible school at their church. My datt did not take well to that.

He had to tell us more than once we were not allowed to go. Then he went to visit our neighbor.

"Ralph, I know you probably didn't mean any harm by inviting my kids, but you shouldn't have brought it up with them without asking me first. Under no circumstances would we allow them to do something like that, and you should know better than to bring it up," my datt said. Things remained a bit tense between them for several weeks. Ralph never invited us again.

———

My parents didn't always pay attention to notices the school sent home with me. Despite numerous letters about the fact that I had failed the periodic vision tests at school, my parents never took me to an eye doctor to have my eyes checked. They asked me if I could see the blackboard, and I said I could. At the time I didn't know most people saw better. So my parents simply ignored the letters about my poor vision. Not until I was in my twenties in college did I learn I had a lazy eye.

The parochial Amish school was built about two miles from my home when I was in fifth grade, and from sixth grade on I went to the one-room schoolhouse with other Amish children. Amish parochial school consisted of about thirty students in eight grades, usually two to four students per grade. We all had the same teacher and sat in the same room, informally divided with the first four grades seated on the left side and the older students on the right.

Class started at 7:30 AM and went until 3:00 PM eight months of the year, with no Easter or Christmas breaks except on the day of the holiday itself. We had the other four months off—except for the never-ending farm work, of course.

Our teacher, Eli Yoder, often started class by reading a hymn or a prayer from the prayer book, or maybe a Bible verse. Classes were taught in English except for German classes. For those, we used a German spelling and reading workbook, though many of the songs and readings were taken from the Bible. Sometimes we split into groups of older and younger students. Other times we worked on individual assignments while the teacher taught a different grade. Often students were called to the board to do work while our classmates took notes.

The lessons included subjects like reading, writing, and arithmetic and applied them to Amish life.

"Albert, come up and solve this word problem on the board, please. Be sure to show your work. A farmer buys 15 pigs for $40 each. He feeds them an average of 200 pounds. He spends $300 per month on feed for five months. He sells the pigs for $300 each and the auctioneer takes 4 percent of the total sale price in fees. What is the farmer's profit?"

In theory, the focus on concrete examples made lessons more practical and applicable to our daily life. In reality, though, I didn't learn much besides some German reading and spelling. We had a few books but didn't learn English grammar, history, science, or social studies; the community didn't consider those subjects important. Once I started college, I learned what a disadvantage this approach was.

My last year in the Amish schoolhouse was eighth grade. In order to satisfy state requirements, I then continued what the school called ninth grade until I was 16 years old, which was another two years for me. Those two years consisted of going to school a half-day on Saturdays when I would review what the classes did during the week, and maybe read a little. Throughout the week I had to keep a diary, detailing riveting tidbits from my daily activities.

"Monday, April 1, 1968: Plowed the field. Then I prepared the field for planting and hauled manure.

"Tuesday, July 9, 1968: We did the second cutting of hay.

"Wednesday, August 14, 1968: We went threshing at the neighbors. I shucked wheat today. Tomorrow we are preparing to do the second cutting of hay at the neighbors.

"Thursday, September 26, 1968: Husked corn. We took the ears off the stalk and tossed them on the wagon. Milked the cows, and looked forward to eating corn on the cob at supper.

"Friday, October 25, 1968: It rained so I repaired harnesses and cleaned the milking stations."

My journal went on and on this way, theoretically to fulfill the requirements of a technical school or apprenticeship until I could get a work permit at age sixteen. On May 15, 1969, I turned sixteen and no longer had to journal: School was officially over and I could get a work permit. Initially, I didn't miss school. I just did what everyone else in my world did.

A DAUGHTER'S PERSPECTIVE

The Amish are not exclusive in making impactful decisions for children who are too young to know better. If you are raised in a culture or country that doesn't teach what the rest of the world is doing or the impact of not doing something — like having a basic education — how can you know it is important?

When education is one of the greatest factors causing the economic divide, I can't help but wonder which other cultures prohibit education in an effort to control their population. If you have to control the population by not allowing them to choose, how much confidence do you have in your beliefs?

I have seen the lack of basic education given in Brazil and the direct impact that has on people here. Those who cannot pay for better education often lack the ability to even compete in a market where they have not had access to learning modern skills around the Internet or digital tools, let alone basic math, reading, and grammar. Not to mention the horrors that have resulted and destroyed the young lives of women around the globe who were not taught sex education so they could recognize and stand up against abuse; understand pregnancy and how they could become pregnant; among other life-altering sexual health decisions that a lack of education never gave them a choice in.

If we believe that freedom and life and liberty is a right - education in all areas must come with that so people can choose the beliefs, ideals, and knowledge they desire to pursue.

In Brazil, as I write this, homeschooling is not allowed, as the government doesn't believe that it will be carried out effectively and that it would further segregate some students. However, how is that different from families that choose to shelter children from diversity and other ideas by putting them in fancy private schools, a social bubble, with an utter lack of diversity? Both produce more questions rather than more answers and lead to clear-cut misconceptions and prejudices.

BURNING DOWN

Our two-story house sat on about one hundred acres of farmland. My datt, with the help of the local Amish community, remodeled and added on to the original building to make room for our thirteen family members. The house expanded to accommodate five bedrooms and a large living room where we could all spend time together.

Adjacent to our house, a mere fifty feet away, was a second two-story building. The first floor had two huge fire pits used during the pig slaughter. On the other side of a wall, an open area housed the clothes-washing area and workspace. Along the back wall of this room ran a spring trough that provided water for washing and keeping food cool.

The second story held what we called the shop where we stored an assortment of tools for repairing farm equipment, especially leather-working tools to mend harnesses and bridles. The tack broke periodically from wear and tear; we always seemed to be repairing something.

For our large family, once a year we slaughtered three or four 220-pound pigs. It was an all-day event. Oftentimes my uncle, Eli Mast, and my memm's sister, Susie, came to help. My uncle had only one arm; the other one had gotten caught in some farm equipment and had to be amputated. Instead of a left arm, he had a hook. As kids, we affectionately called him One-armed Eli—but only behind his back. He was a lot of fun.

Slaughter days typically occurred in the fall as the air started to turn crisp. First, we lit the fire pits, burning kindling and dry lumber we had collected from the nearby woods. Then we put two giant kettles of water on the fire to boil.

My datt slaughtered the pigs outside—first shooting them in the head with his rifle, then immediately stabbing them in the jugular vein to drain the blood, letting it soak into the earth. The jugular needed to be pierced immediately after shooting the pig, so the heart kept beating to drain as much blood as possible from the carcass until reality caught up with it. The pig was then rolled onto two large ropes with which four strong men hoisted it into a large trough.

By then the water was boiling over the fire pits. Two strong boys inserted a wooden rod under the handle to carry it to the trough and pour the water over the pig. The carcass was rolled around in the scalding water, sizzling until we smelled the burning hair. Then the pig was moved onto a wooden platform, where it was scrubbed and shaved under additional scalding water to clean off any remaining dirt and hair. Once the pigskin was stripped raw and pink, it was ready to be gutted.

All the internal organs were removed, including the intestines, to be saved and eaten in some fashion. The intestines were cleaned and later boiled to create the thin film used for sausage casing. Intestinal casing made the sausage especially delicious, though much sausage casing today is artificial.

Next, the pig was quartered and taken inside the shed, where the meat was separated from the bones. The hindquarters were soaked in a vat of water to salt cure. My datt added salt to the water until an egg floated on top. Later, on smoking day, we burned hickory wood to smoke the meat. Then the smoked meat was hung in the basement of the house until we were ready to eat it.

Smaller pieces of meat my memm canned for later use. The rest of the meat was ground up and fed through a machine that pumped it into the intestinal casing to make juicy rolls of sausage. The bones we tossed into the trash.

The fire roared through most of the day—first to boil the water for scalding, then for cooking the meat, and lastly for my favorite part, making pork rinds. Pork rinds are fried pig skin, sometimes called chitlins. The chitlins were always best when still hot, just cooled enough to not burn my tongue. One of my jobs was to cut the skin into one-inch squares and toss them into a pot. We scooped them out and ate them like French fries. The fat left behind, known as lard, settled to the bottom of the pot. My mother scooped that out to save for making her delicious pie crusts and baked goods.

The slaughter of 1967 was one of our most memorable. Preparing the meat had gone just like every other year— hard labor with the benefit of delicious foods stockpiled for the coming winter. After a long day of sausage making and meat processing, our bellies were full of pork rinds. We ate a light supper, finished our chores, and went to bed.

About midnight, my memm heard a noise and saw a light in the kitchen that scared her. She woke my datt up and sent him to investigate. My room faced the shed, but my brothers and I were sound asleep, unaware of the impending danger, with no idea that the outside wall had already started to blister from the heat. My datt walked outside, rubbing the sleep from his eyes before reality dawned on him.

In a panic, he shouted, "Fire!

Kids!

Wake up!"

We woke to the sound of horses galloping outside our window. However, it wasn't horses, it was a raging fire. The light was intensely bright and mere feet from our bedroom. The roof of the shed was already collapsing. Panic ensued— on our feet in seconds, we shouted and screamed. We threw on some clothing and ran outside.

"Grab water from the troughs, boys! Throw it on the fire! Jacob, run to Ralph Kaser's and have him call the fire department."

My brother raced across the fields to our neighbor's house. The rest of us lined up in a bucket brigade to throw water on the shed, but buckets of water were of little use against a roaring blaze.

Jacob returned with Ralph, who came to help. When they arrived, my datt thought we had it under control. He realized that the shed was lost and we could do nothing about it, and assumed the worst was over.

"You can call the fire department off, Ralph," Datt said.

"Samuel, they're already on their way. And you're going to need them," said Ralph, grabbing a bucket. Our water had created billows of smoke, but the fire was still burning.

In short order, two fire trucks with tanks showed up; like most Amish, we didn't have a fire hydrant. By the time the fire department arrived the roof of the shed had fallen in.

One fireman asked, "Where can we fill the tanks with water?"

Datt pointed at the pond. The fire chief spoke with him as the rest of the team set up the hoses.

"Sir, we'll try to save your house. If it catches, though, it'll be tough to put out," he said. Datt looked a bit surprised since the house wasn't on fire, but he quickly understood. In the frenzy of the moment, he hadn't considered the impact of the intense heat.

In small-town America, shared knowledge in difficult situations, even among different cultures, is essential, and the local community often goes beyond mere courtesy to help each other out. Our English neighbor, Ralph, recognized the danger to our house, and thanks to his insight we were not left homeless. The Amish community relies on members in group projects called frolics, where the whole community comes together and can build a barn or a house in a couple of days. In the same way, local communities work together to support each other, both within the Amish and beyond, to provide help and support amid tragic events, difficult crop harvests, and terrible weather, crossing boundaries between cultures to help out a friendly neighbor.

Because the shed was right next to the house, the walls

were already starting to blister from the heat. The shed was lost, but the house was salvageable. Rather than trying to put out the existing fire, which had mostly burned down to a smolder, the firefighters hosed off the house to cool it down so it wouldn't catch fire.

When the fire had dwindled to mere puffs and gasps of smoke, the closest wall was blistered from the heat but appeared free of flames. The firemen went to inspect our house thoroughly, both inside and out, to ensure the fire wasn't burning inside the walls. Fortunately, they found no live embers. We felt blessed to have at least saved our house.

If Memm hadn't woken up and heard the fire, all of us boys, who were sound sleepers, likely would never have woken up. Our room would have been one of the first places to burn.

The fire department determined that the likely cause was a bird's nest in the shed's chimney that had ignited during the sausage-making and pig slaughter. When we went to bed that night, the fire was probably already burning. It must have been burning for quite a while for Memm to wake up to the roar of it.

We lost all of the meat from that slaughter and most of our tools, but we rebuilt the shed, adding a separate shop and tool shed, farther from the house to prevent a recurrence.

Almost nothing was salvageable because of the heat. Everything metal melted into a twisted puddle, and the leather harnesses were unrecognizable.

ELI AND THE PONY

When I was about ten and Eli was fifteen, he went out for a pleasant day of riding. Unfortunately, the pony had other plans. Ponies tend to be more mischievous than horses and are often more stubborn and difficult to train. Training ponies to follow the rider's orders can be surprisingly difficult.

On this particular day the pony, which was a young colt still in training, decided to test my brother. The pony refused to listen to Eli's instructions, determined to do what he wanted instead, while Eli clung to his back, trying to stay on. The pony ran toward the barn, out of control. Clean milk cans had been set on an elevated stand next to the barn, waiting for the milkman to pick them up. The pony raced up to the stand and bucked, kicking his back legs into the air and throwing my brother right into the milk stand. Then the pony sauntered off as if nothing had happened, leaving my brother in tears. Eli's arm was seriously twisted and crooked. The accident scared all of us, but none so much as Eli.

The pony had deliberately thrown Eli off, resulting in him suffering a broken arm. Datt took Eli over to Ralph Kaser's house to get them a ride to the hospital. Before he left, he spoke with Mose and Jacob.

"Take the pony up to the field we just plowed, where the ground is soft and ready to be planted. Ride him hard until he breaks. If he bucks you off there, it won't hurt. We'll be back as soon as we can. Show him who is the boss."

"We can do that, Datt!" The boys seemed happy to head out to the fields to show the pony who was boss.

I was too young to help but walked up to the field to watch my two older brothers break in the pony. Mose and Jacob rode the pony over and over, taking turns and not letting him stop until he was worn out and sweaty.

Questioning authority was not tolerated on the farm. One small act of rebellion from the pony, and he was taught his lesson. My brothers slowly wore down any thoughts the pony had of doing things differently. The breaking in of an animal is a lot like the breaking down of the human spirit. You can only take so much negativity before, like it or not, you eventually give in. The only question left is, how long can your soul hold out against unrelenting coercion?

Eli spent a couple of months with his arm in a cast. But that pony never bucked any of us again. He had learned his lesson that he could buck all he wanted, but in the end, people were in charge.

HORSE AND LIVESTOCK AUCTIONS

Farmerstown, about six miles from our farm, held a weekly local livestock auction. We went there to sell our pigs or beef cattle when they were ready for market. My datt also bought piglets and beef calves to raise.

Ralph Kaser worked at the auction, so he often took my datt's livestock to market in his truck. And when my datt needed to buy something, he went to auction with Mr. Kaser. As kids, we always argued among ourselves about who would get to go with him.

Johnny Andrews, the owner of the livestock facilities, was a gifted auctioneer. I loved sitting and listening to him sell item after item with his rapid-fire speech. The words ran together so fast, they seemed to buzz like the soft hum of bees making honey, culminating in an exaggerated "Sold!" as he banged his gavel.

The range of animals sold at these auctions was extensive and varied week to week, depending on the season. There might be fattened pigs ready to slaughter, or piglets to be raised and sold at a future auction. Beef cattle and dairy cows were regular features.

My datt went to auction a couple of times a year. When we were small, he might take one or two of us at a time, but once we got older we were all allowed to tag along since he didn't need to watch us and we wouldn't get in the way. The actual auction usually faded into the background as we sought out the friends and neighbors we didn't get to see often.

At these events, we hoped to get something bought, which was an uncommon treat for us. If we were lucky, my datt bought us a hot dog, a root beer or a Coke, or maybe even ice cream. The scarcity of bought things didn't seem like a lack to us; it only made those occasions that much more of a treat.

Growing up we never felt poor. We never lacked food or clothing to wear and rarely went out to eat. Most of what we ate and used on a daily basis came from the farm or was exchanged among community members. We might buy hot dogs at the auction, or stop for a burger in town after a trip to the doctor's office. Such extravagances are more common among the Amish today.

Twice a year horses were bought and sold at auction. Many of the horses brought to the sale were retired racehorses or those that didn't perform well at the racetrack. The Amish bought them to pull their buggies. Most of the field horses were bred, raised, bought, and sold within the community.

Horse auctions were big community events, and we were always thrilled, competing especially hard with our siblings to go with Datt those days. I remember riding in the back of Ralph Kaser's livestock truck, standing up and holding on to the rails as we drove through the countryside.

SUICIDE

In every culture of the world, funerals are an important event. Among the Amish, funerals were a time to come together as a community, visit with family and friends, and remember the life of a loved one who had gone to heaven.

Funerals of older people, those who had already lived a full life, were typically sorrowful events. The Amish celebrated a farewell ceremony, similar to the Catholic last rites, for people at the end of their lives. As the shadow of death approached, they still had time to visit with family and friends before death stole away their last breath.

Family members and neighbors got together to sing and pray for a peaceful end, reminding each other that they would all meet again in heaven. Though these occasions were sad, they provided a sense of closure. Tears were stifled in order to look strong and because deep down everyone believed that death will carry the person to a better place. Those farewell ceremonies were nothing compared to the deaths of those who died unexpectedly.

Sudden deaths—a healthy person injured in an accident, or victim of a sudden illness—had no final farewell. The sorrow of such funerals seemed to permeate the very walls of the room where friends and family gathered to say their last goodbyes.

Very rarely, Amish children died before they were a member of the church, usually because they were too young to join. Or perhaps a young adult had put off the decision to join, or worse yet was on suspension for not following the rules. Small children were not considered accountable; the Amish believe they are innocent and have an automatic ticket to heaven. However, for young adults of the age where their peers joined the church and they had not, the Amish find it hard to accept that they will be allowed into heaven—they understood the choice but had not yet confessed their faith.

Most funerals were rather uneventful for me. I considered

them a more somber version of family reunions. That was, until the funeral of Jonas Yoder.

Jonas had been the bishop of our church district for as long as my twelve-year-old self could remember. He worked closely with my datt, who was the deacon. Deacons are influencers, the strong arm of the bishop to enforce church rules. It was a shock to our entire community when Jonas, in his mid-forties, died by his own hand.

Suicide is no less common among the Amish than in the general population, although for many Amish, it would be harder to leave the community than to die by suicide. Most Amish love their lives, but for those who don't fit in, they often see no other choice. Simply leaving the community isn't considered an option.

Even among those who suffer from depression, suicide is still rare. The Amish church considers it a sin, teaching that those who die by suicide go to hell and must be buried outside the cemetery fence.

One blustery spring day a fellow church member knocked on our door.

"*Albaht, ish da datt dehiem?*" (Albert, is your dad at home?)

"*Yah, ich grek iehn fahdich*" (Yes, I'll get him for you.)

The men went out to the barn to talk in private. After about twenty minutes, Datt came back to the house to grab his coat and traveling hat. Tears ran down the cheeks of his saddened face—an unnerving sight on a man who never cried.

"Jonas Yoder is very ill and in the hospital. A group of us are going up to see him." He turned and left without another word. The neighbor who had been out on the porch didn't go to the hospital with my datt, so he stayed and told us what had happened.

"Seems Jonas tried to kill himself."

The words seemed to cut a bite out of time. The world stopped moving for minutes that felt like hours.

What am I supposed to think when the head of the church attempts a mortal sin?

"Gunshot to the head. He's unresponsive, in a coma," the man whispered into the still air.

What would make a person want to do that? Was there a fight?

My next thought went to his kids. The oldest was a bit older than me, about sixteen, and some were closer to my age.

What do you do when you hear a gunshot from the basement of the house?

I wondered if the family had anticipated finding him lying in a pool of his own blood.

My datt and the other preachers practically lived at the hospital for the better part of a week, praying for him. Jonas regained consciousness briefly and was able to speak with them the day before he died, asking forgiveness for his sin. The church leaders were relieved by his repentance since in the Amish tradition you need only be aware and petition for forgiveness for it to be offered. Since he had been forgiven for his sin, he could be buried in the cemetery.

Datt finally came home and told us, "He passed peacefully into the next life and was forgiven."

I felt really sorry for Jonas's kids, who would have to carry on the farm work without a father, with no real guidance, the person they had looked up to, their hero, who had taken his own life.

How will that change their lives?

Over the next months and years, they seemed to grow up strong and the farm prospered. I couldn't help pondering, *What went on in their minds after that?*

The day of the funeral was nice and sunny, but as friends and relatives gathered the mood was unusually somber. This wasn't just any funeral, but that of a suicide victim who was a respected leader of the church. The sorrow on people's faces was more evident than at other funerals I had attended.

Like any other funeral, it started early in the morning with singing and sermons, which were a part of a eulogy. It was clear that it was difficult for the preacher tasked with the sermon to deliver those words, as everyone there wished this funeral wasn't happening. The weight of circumstances was no less on the preacher's mind than of those in attendance.

Nevertheless, the funeral sermon took an optimistic tone, expressing hope that Jonas would go to heaven because he had been forgiven.

"If we could all be like children, then we would all be forgiven and go to heaven," the preacher intoned.

When it came time to walk past the open casket—a plain pine box—and say our final goodbyes, I saw far more tears and crying than at most funerals. The other preachers from Jonas`s district, who were like brothers to him, felt the loss as deeply as the family members.

Then the casket was taken by horse-drawn buggy to the cemetery, where friends and relatives sang and prayed again. The sadness and silence felt heavier than usual as everyone hitched up their buggies and headed home. In the silence, more was spoken than could have been put into words.

That was when the first questions about life and death entered my mind.

Maybe I should kill myself now, while I'm still a kid. What if I do something wrong as an adult? At least now I know I'd go to heaven.

My brain quickly worked through various scenarios to save my soul through an early and untimely death.

From the hayloft? With a rope? I could jump as it pulled tight.

My brother Jacob found me a few days later standing on a beam in the barn, contemplating these thoughts. At that point, I was merely thinking about the idea and looking at sites and options. I was never depressed to the point that I didn't want to live, even as I considered how I could end my life. These thoughts were more about a way to guarantee that I would go to heaven. I didn't have a bad life growing up. We lived a simple life, but we had plenty to eat, plenty of fun, siblings, and security. Sure, my siblings and I quarreled and had spats, but it was a good life.

"*Vas bischt du am duah?*" (What are you doing?) Jacob jolted me out of my morbid daze.

Finally, I replied, "*Ich bein ischt ahm ruhm gooka!*" (I'm just looking around!)

The interruption opened my eyes to suicide. *Duh, Albert,*

44

you know better. If you kill yourself, you'll go to hell anyway.

I never thought about suicide again. If you know better and you do the wrong thing, it is still wrong. It doesn't matter if you are a child or a member of the church already.

That was when I realized that the choice was no longer between going to heaven and leaving the community to sort things out. *What if I was wrong and went to hell anyway?* I had to face my doubts about the Amish religion and my community in real life. Escaping to heaven early was not an option.

A DAUGHTER'S REFLECTION

One of the things I have always loved about the Amish is the sense of community and family. Especially growing up with limited contact with much of my extended family, I thought it was so fun to go as a kid to the large gatherings to be surrounded by people who you knew deep down are all looking out for each other, not just one or two but literally hundreds.

The importance of community can be felt by all - when we lack it - in those moments of pain and agony when you have to cry alone or don't have a helping hand to turn to. You wonder, are there other people out there facing what I'm going through?

Community is essential to survival. While you don't

have to be Amish to have a community, they do have the concept right. For hundreds of years, they have fostered a community that shares the good times and the bad. A community that helps solve difficult problems with emotional, spiritual, and at times financial help to assure that members do not feel alone. The quest for the right community throughout life is essential to living a life that feels fulfilled.

MILLER HOMECOMINGS

Growing up Amish wasn't all hard work and frustration; in fact, we often had a lot of fun. The Amish community truly believes in the ideals of community and helping out neighbors and family. We always had family members and neighbors around to relax and enjoy free time with.

My favorite annual event as a child was the Miller Homecoming. Every summer in June, after the busy planting season and before the even busier harvest season, all the brothers and sisters in my father's family along with all their children got together for a reunion. Each member of the family took turns hosting. My grandpa on my datt's side died when I was about six, and my grandma a few years later, so they weren't part of the Miller Homecomings for most of the years that I remember. But we had tons of cousins, aunts, and uncles. One of my favorite characters was Pudding Joe, my datt's youngest brother, who could eat more pudding than anyone I ever knew!

We played a lot of sports at these gatherings and softball was a favorite. When I was young, the cousins played against the uncles. As we grew up and the uncles got older, we started choosing teams of cousins while the older generation sat and watched. The girls helped to prepare the food for lunch, sat around talking, and sometimes even joined in the softball game with the boys.

The women of the family spent most of the day in the kitchen cooking and preparing for the event. One thing we never lacked was food. Every family brought a dish to the meal, although the host was responsible for the main dishes like the meats. Meals included glazed ham, roasted chicken, mashed potatoes, mac and cheese, buttered noodles, homemade applesauce, a variety of jellos with fruit, veggie salad, cakes, pies, cookies, and so much more.

And no Miller Homecoming was complete without ice cream in the middle of the afternoon. The ice cream helped us cool down after a tough softball game. When Uncle Albert, who owned a harness shop in New Bedford next to the general store, hosted the reunion, he bought ice cream by the gallon. Otherwise, we made hand-cranked ice cream. We all took turns cranking the ice cream maker with chunks of ice to turn creamy milk into rich, delicious ice cream. Every Miller family had a freezer for ice cream, usually kept cold with blocks of ice. We made vanilla or chocolate, sometimes adding fruits like strawberries or bananas. Sometimes we topped it with Cheerios, along with chocolate, butterscotch, or caramel sauces. Ice cream has always been a Miller family tradition.

We also had an annual Barkman reunion, but that was smaller since my memm had only three brothers and one sister. The Barkman Homecoming didn't compare to my datt's family, with his seven brothers and one sister plus their families. The events were pretty much the same, however, the Miller side was more fun with more people.

A DAUGHTER'S RETURN

In 2019 my now-adult sisters and I attended the Miller Homecoming with my dad. Everything at our grandpa's old house looked at once familiar and different. A third house on the property, built about five years ago for my unmarried aunt, wasn't there when we visited as kids. Esther had spent years caring for her parents and now had a place to call her own. She served me tea in her garden and gave me a tour.

The new modernized shed where the buggies used to be kept was almost empty except for rows of benches and long tables laden with food against the wall. The women sat on one side of the shed with the men on the other side. The division was not too strict; family members mingled and conversations flowed throughout the room.

My dad, stepmom, and sisters went to talk to some

of my uncles while I sat down to catch up with some cousins and aunts.

"Do you remember me?" they all asked.

I recognized most of the faces but struggled to pull out some of the names, especially ones I didn't see often while growing up—thirty-plus women! They had changed a good deal since we were children, now all the adult women had a baby on their hip - either their own or a grandchild.

Mary, who used to babysit me, and her sister seemed hesitant to approach me at first. I realized they wanted to ask something but weren't sure whether they should. Like cousins everywhere, they asked anyway.

"How's your mom? She was always nice to us. I wonder about her..." Since my dad remarried over twenty years ago, I knew why they hesitated to ask.

"Honestly, I haven't seen her in over fifteen years. She barely speaks to any of us," I said.

"Oh, sure, I understand. We know people like that. I'm sorry to hear that," said Mary. Giggling a bit, she added, "Now, I don't want to be rude, but can I ask you something?"

I assumed the question was something else about my mom. "Of course."

"Is that your real hair color? We obviously have redheads in our family." She laughed, fingering her own bright red hair. "It's just that I remember you being blonder as a kid."

Laughing off the tension over my mom, I said, "No, you're right, I dye it. I've always preferred being a redhead."

"Well, it suits you. It looks natural."

Once the ice was broken, we chatted about life in the past and what was current in our lives. Mary who was only a couple of years older than me was already a grandmother, while I was still considering my own children in the future.

I remembered past events being far quieter. No one ever seemed to make much of an effort to talk to us, but this time everyone was very friendly. I bounced from one conversation to the next, finding it easy to talk with my aunts and cousins about my job as a teacher. Plus we compared our different lifestyles, and I shared differences between Ohio and Brazil. Most of the cousins my age had between three and eight children, and the fact that I didn't even have a current boyfriend got just a gentle nod and reassurance that I would find someone, with none of the judgment I got from other people.

Uncle John's eldest son pulled out of his wallet a picture of his two children taken at the local Walmart to show me how much they had grown. When I was a child, pictures of the Amish, even of family, were practically forbidden, and even still they are rare. In a world focused on Instagram and social media self-promotion that borderlines on narcissism, I can't help but think that perhaps the Amish got the idea of less is more when it comes to photography of people right. Some memories are best remembered as echoes on the soul rather than posted and reposted for others' approval.

My immediate family was put first in line for the

food and encouraged to sit with the men. My dad's brothers talked with us to catch up on our lives. Even Andy, the one brother-in-law my dad had had the most issues with in the past, was open and friendly.

When we finished eating, my uncles took us all on a tour to see how the pond and back area of the farm had changed since their youth. For my dad, the farm looked quite different, meanwhile, I had trouble picturing him ice skating on the pond and getting cold water from a now-dilapidated building.

We didn't play any softball at this reunion, though some of the younger kids got a game of tetherball going. The right players of diverse ages just weren't invested in the game that year. So by late afternoon, we headed out, but not without exchanging a few addresses to keep in contact.

We didn't return home right from the reunion but instead went to a neighboring relative's house for a buggy ride. My youngest sister had asked for one in jest and got what she asked for. She likely didn't remember the rides we used to go on in my childhood, since she was very young when we moved farther away from our relatives' farms. I used to love having our cousins drive us around their farms in the horse and buggy.

My dad took the reins like a pro and drove us down the street while my stepmom and sisters giggled in semi-nervousness. They were afraid dad had forgotten how to drive a horse, but the horse knew what to do. Besides, like a bicycle, once someone learns to drive a buggy, they never forget.

I often wish I could connect more with my roots, but at the same time my path has led me to another part of the world, and I love where it has taken me. Perhaps in the future, I can reconnect more deeply with family.

HORSING AROUND

When I was seventeen, not long before I left the Amish community, I was out doing chores with my datt. My younger siblings were at school and my older siblings had their own jobs or farms.

My datt licked his finger and held it up to the wind. He had long since taught me this trick for telling when rain was on the way. He looked west and then south, watching for a change in the weather. Even the clouds looked unsettled, rolling and seething overhead.

"I need to go to New Bedford this morning. It's going to rain this evening and we need to get the fields planted before then. I want you to go up to the fields on the hill that are already plowed and get them ready for me to seed this afternoon when I get back. After you finish up there, I want you to start preparing the field near the barn, and I'll plant that in the afternoon, too."

"Yes, sir," I said, always the dutiful son.

I hitched up a four-horse team to pull the heavy disc-harrow. With a four-horse team, I drove the two horses in the center. The two outside horses were hooked to the center pair and simply followed their lead. The disc-harrow readied the plowed field for planting by making the soil soft and even.

I finished the first fields easily and still had time left before lunch, so I headed toward the field next to the barn. To get there from the hill I had to cross a pasture. I drove the team, still hitched to the disc-harrow, up to the pasture gate, stopped the team, and went to open the gate, as I had done countless times before. This time, though, as I hopped down to swing the gate open, something unsettled the horses. Perhaps it was my sudden movement or some sound I didn't hear. Next thing I knew the horses had bolted toward me, pulling the disc-harrow behind them. I ran directly into their path to try to stop them.

"Hoo hoo, stop, boys." Normally the horses easily stop at this command, but they were coming too fast to stop in time and my back was up against the fence. I jumped to the side and got out of the way just in time. The outside horse swerved and nearly hit me.

"Neeeiiigh!" he whinnied in fear. He reared up on his hind legs, giving me a few seconds before impact. Instinctively, I dove under his front legs into a rolling somersault, barely avoiding the flailing hooves. The horse was not so lucky.

In his effort to avoid trampling me, he lost his balance against the lead horses that were pulling him to the right. His foot slipped and he went down on his side. The rest of the team dragged the poor animal like a sack of grain along the side of the disc-harrow. They were in full panic now and stampeded directly toward a tree, veering off only when the disc-harrow hit the tree. The harness broke, freeing the horses from each other. Once they all realized they were free from both the weight and the reins, their panic eased. The startled horses stopped running and started to calm down. The fallen horse struggled to his feet. The first thing he did, after being dragged by a team of runaways, was come back to check on me.

All of this happened in less than thirty seconds. I lay on the ground covered in dirt, grass, and tears of terror. Slowly all four horses came back and stood around me, heads bowed as if in a silent prayer I couldn't hear through my sobs. Rolling around in my head was still the shock and fear of knowing that I had nearly been trampled. I would never have survived the weight of a full-grown horse on my chest. The horses watched, calm now as I climbed to my feet.

Eventually, they scattered into the pasture and meandered back to the barn. I brushed off my clothes and gathered up chunks of the shattered disc-harrow. Back at the barn, I patted the horses and thanked them for not trampling me as I unharnessed them and put them in their stalls to rest.

Then I went back to the gate to collect the rest of the ruined equipment. The disc was badly dented. The hitching post lay in pieces under the maple tree, now scarred from the incident. Not a single piece of the harness was intact. I took the broken pieces back and started to repair what I could.

When my datt returned from town, he found me working on the broken harness.

"What happened?" he asked sharply.

I recounted the tale as accurately as possible, still shaken by the incident and covered in dirt and grass.

"Why can't I count on you for anything...?" His words stung. At first, I took the verbal lashing in silence, but then his lack of empathy gave me the courage to speak up.

"A half-hour ago I felt lucky to be alive, now I'm not so sure. The disc almost ran over me! At least the horses had the sense to try to avoid me. That's why everything is broken. I wasn't hurt, and neither were the horses. Thanks for not caring enough to ask. The harnesses we can fix. The first field is ready for you to plant. The only problem is that we can't plant the second field today."

My datt was a tough man and could be harsh, but he was also a good and honest man. I could tell my words made him think. Most of the harnesses we couldn't repair on our own, but he helped me patch together those we could use to finish that day's planting. The rest needed to go to my uncle's harness shop to be restitched. The collars and leather seams must be able to hold up against thousands of pounds of horses and equipment, and they require much more work than simply piecing them back together by hand.

———

Some thirty years later my brother-in-law Mose Yoder, who took over my datt's farm, decided to give up farming. He auctioned off the equipment he had used on our homestead farm, and I happened to be visiting during the event. With a wink and a chuckle Mose said, "Just a second, Albert, I got something to show you."

He led me over to the row of farm equipment lined up for sale. When he reached the disc-harrow he leaned over and pointed to the dent.

"Remind you of anything, Albert?" he joked.

It's amazing, and even a little funny, how life-and-death moments rife with terror can fade into a mere whisper with time.

RUMSPRINGA

When I was growing up, young children, even boys, typically wore a dress until they were out of diapers for the mother's convenience in changing diapers. As we grew, we shifted to the traditional Amish garb—handmade shirts with three or four buttons, wide-brimmed hats, and suspenders. The first big step into manhood was being allowed to go without suspenders. The age to go suspender-less varied from community to community but usually was about fourteen. It was the first step into adulthood—but the custom that every Amish kid longed for was Rumspringa.

Rumspringa is translated as *running around* but is more accurately described as the dating phase of Amish life. Rumspringa doesn't condone any wild or crazy behavior, as often depicted in the media. Rather, it is more about hanging out with friends and attending singings. Rumspringa usually starts at age sixteen and continues until marriage, which typically occurs sometime in the early twenties. I entered Rumspringa after my sixteenth birthday.

Most communities had one person who cut people's hair. My datt usually cut my hair, in a long straight bowl-cut, the traditional Amish style. During Rumspringa, boys often cut their hair shorter in what was called a fancy haircut. The new haircut helped mark boys as being in Rumspringa and thus open for dates. I was proud of my first fancy haircut— short and tapered. Naturally, my datt did not approve, and a scolding always followed any time I got my hair cut.

During Rumspringa I was allowed to go to singings, where youth got together to sing songs and hang out. They were held on Sunday evenings when the week's church service host had Rumspringa-age children. Since singings didn't occur every week, we often went to a neighboring church district, and in turn, their youth visited ours, allowing for wider exposure to potential dates.

On Wednesday evenings boys in Rumspringa gathered at some designated local area, usually a community store, and made plans for what to do on the upcoming Saturday and Sunday nights. We talked about singings and whether we had a date, and sometimes did "boy things" like play cards or drink soda. Often I was too busy on the farm to attend these hangouts.

Saturday and Sunday were date nights. Amish boys didn't directly ask girls out on dates. Instead, I would have a friend ask the desired girl out on a date on my behalf. The tradition made it easier for the girl to say no if she wasn't interested in a particular boy, without fear of offending him.

My neighbor, Atlee Yoder, and I were best buddies. I also ran around with Mose Yoder, who eventually married my sister Anna and is now my brother-in-law. Atlee and I worked together to ask girls out for each other, always trying to get a date for every Saturday night. Guys who didn't have a date frequently engaged in harmless mischief.

Boys typically started dating as soon as they entered Rumspringa at age 16, dated multiple girls (at the same time) for a while, and had a steady girlfriend by 18 or 19. It may sound rather promiscuous, but the practice was designed to keep kids at home, out of trouble, and in the Amish fold.

Once a couple had dated for a while, they considered going steady. In the Amish community, a couple who decided to go steady usually intended to get married. It wasn't common for steady couples to break up, though it did happen occasionally.

When I had a date on a Saturday, after my chores were done I got cleaned up before hitching up the buggy and driving to the girl's house by 8:00 or 9:00 PM. By that time everyone else in the household was likely already in bed since most Amish fieldwork starts at 4:30 or 5:00 AM. I pulled my buggy up to the house and put the horse in an open stall for the night. No one expected me to ring the doorbell or even knock. The door was always left open. Even if I had never been to the house before I could find the girl's room; hers was usually the only upstairs light left on in the house, like a beacon. I had to climb the stairs past her parents' room on the first floor. Usually, you didn't see any other family members unless there were more teenage siblings in the home.

My date and I would spend the night together. This practice started both to avoid the long drive back home in the middle of the night and so young people didn't go out to do more 'worldly' activities. We stayed up to chat a long time, then cuddled up and slept in the same bed. Sometimes clothes stayed on all night, other times not. We didn't have a lot of other recreational options, certainly couldn't go to a restaurant or the movies, and had only limited time to spend alone together to get to know each other. We talked about everything and quickly became close. In the morning before everyone else got up, I crawled out of bed and went home. Sometimes I ran into her father starting his chores for the day as I hitched up the horse. Then I would politely say hello before heading on my way.

No one in the girl's house bothered a couple on a date. To keep young people from being tempted to go somewhere just to have some privacy, families left them alone to help keep them Amish, even though the practice may seem contrary to other traditional religious beliefs.

It was a question of trust. The community trusted the young couple to uphold Amish values and traditions and wait to explore sexuality until after marriage. Though neither the Amish culture nor religion encourages premarital sex, Amish youth do have sex, probably at a similar rate as the rest of the teenage population. Sex was certainly more common after a couple started going steady.

So, why weren't all Amish girls pregnant at sixteen? Amish youth learned about sex early on from the farm animals. Condoms were available to prevent pregnancy; though birth control pills may be more common now.

Occasionally a pregnancy did occur, but not often, and when it did the couple usually got married. If not, children born out of wedlock were often raised by the girl's parents although they knew who their memm was. Premarital pregnancy among the Amish does not have the stigma found so often in English society. Such children were part of the central family as much as any other child. If the mother got married later, the child would go live with her.

During Rumspringa the youth are not yet church members and are not governed by the church rules. Some of my friends had radios and liked to listen to the Cleveland Indians games. For some parents, a radio wasn't a big deal. But if my datt had ever found me with one, the radio would have gone under a sledgehammer. As a deacon, the church leader who enforced church doctrine, Datt didn't take kindly to his children breaking the rules.

Even though I knew both the rules and the risks, I saved my money and bought a little 9-volt transistor radio. For me, ten dollars was a lot of money; back then a soda cost twenty-five cents. I only got spending money on special occasions like hanging out with the other boys on Wednesdays or going to the auction with Datt. I kept my radio hidden under the hay in the barn and only took it out on Saturdays when I had a date. I thought listening to the radio was a great way to impress a girl.

———

After long days working in the field, it wasn't unusual for me to fall asleep on the drive home from a singing. The horses knew the way and I trusted them to get me home safely. More than once I woke up from a nice nap to find the horse waiting patiently in front of our barn.

One evening I was startled awake by the sound of gunshots. I looked around in a panic, with no idea where I was except that it wasn't home. An electric light on a pole stood in the yard, so I knew it wasn't any other Amish home either.

My first instinct was to get out of there and fast. I slapped the reins on the horse's back and hauled it back toward the road. Once there I got my bearings; my horse had inadvertently taken me to the Lauer farm, two farms before our house.

The Lauers were not as friendly as our other neighbors. They weren't happy to have a buggy pull up to their house in the middle of the night and just sit there as I dozed in the driver's seat.

I'm sure they didn't think I was coming to do them harm. If I'd wanted to rob them, a horse and buggy surely wasn't the stealthiest approach.

————

When I wasn't too busy with planting or harvest, I spent Wednesday and Saturday evenings in the village at Beck's Mill or in New Bedford, playing cards and talking with my friends. We weren't supposed to use the king, queen, and jack face cards, but we did anyway.

When I wasn't on a date, like most teenage boys, I liked a good laugh. Even harmless pranks were always a risk for me since my datt was the deacon and well known in my church and neighboring communities.

On some Saturdays, my group was more mischievous than others. One of my favorite pranks was "Buggy in the Stall". At community gatherings, visitors put their horses in a stall and left the buggy parked outside. It took four of us to quietly roll the closest buggy into the milking station, which had bent pipes that confined the cow during milking. Two of us removed a wheel in turn and put the axle through the pipes while the other two held the buggy up, then reattached the wheel to the axle. The prank was impossible to undo alone, so the unlucky owner of the buggy had to admit he had been pranked and ask for help getting it out again.

We stood by, watching and trying not to laugh as we waited for the owner to realize he couldn't get his buggy out of the barn. He looked puzzled and then went back to the house, grinning.

"Seems my buggy's gone off and tried to get itself milked," he said with a sheepish smile. "Could I get some help?"

We snickered and ran off to watch from a distance as the men liberated the buggy, recounting their own Rumspringa pranks. Our pranks could be annoying and take up time, but they were never destructive, as that went against our values as a community.

Our best prank, though, involved the invisible cows. One Saturday night one of my friends said, "Let's play a prank on Mr. Yoder."

I didn't think Mr. Yoder, not a member of our local district, knew me or my friends because by buggy it took the better part of an hour to get to his place from my house.

I drew the short straw. Mustering up my courage, I steadied the flashlight in my hand and went up to knock on Mr. Yoder's door.

I said, "Excuse me, sir, but I think your cows are out. These are your cows in the pasture, right?"

"Yeah."

"Well, some of them are on the road."

"OK, son, thanks for letting me know. I'll go get dressed."

He came out with a Coleman lantern and walked all over but saw no cows anywhere on the road. He finally turned back to his property and found all his cows in the pasture, right where they belonged. If the cows had been out, we would have helped him corral them, but instead, we sat in our buggy and watched him wander around while we laughed and laughed.

Mr. Yoder was pretty sure that the boy who knocked on his door was one of Sam Miller's sons. A few days later my datt asked if my friends and I had played a prank on Mr. Yoder.

"How did you know? I didn't think Mr. Yoder knew me."

My datt had already guessed my answer. I saw a twinge of a smile on his face. "You know us, Millers, we all have the same look. Mr. Yoder said thanks for not actually letting his cows out."

———

Some Amish youth also experimented with alcohol during Rumspringa. When we got a little older and felt reckless, three or four boys piled into a buggy together and headed to a bar in Baltic called Schlarb's. At the time the legal drinking age for 3.2 percent beer was only eighteen. We sat at the bar drinking together, not socializing with English people, and then went home.

Once we even bought a case of beer to take to a singing. It was summer, and naturally, the buggy had no refrigeration. An ice chest was an impossibility. Cheap warm beer never did anyone any good. We took it out at the singing to share with the other boys; the girls didn't usually drink.

That night I threw up and I had a terrible hangover the next day. Beer wasn't nearly as glamorous as I expected.

A DAUGHTER'S COMING OF AGE

The modern focus on 'likes' and one's image is exhausting. I long for the times when people focused more on the quality of your character than on if you had enough social influence and looked good. Especially as a girl who always preferred sports to dresses, it is hard to stand my ground and be me in a world focused on looking like Barbie.

The tedious focus on garnishing images of oneself or one's life for a sense of reassurance from others is something that has become a disease in our society. Instead of focusing on real traits and characteristics, people have become so superficial that they do not bother to gain real knowledge and often cannot even stick to their own values. Instead of building oneself to be the best person possible, people have been striving to create the best 'fake' image possible – an online life without problems – an impossible life to obtain. As they see this reflected in others' social images, everyday people feel they are failures for the ups and downs that naturally happen in life. Instead of reaching out to their community and focusing on building that and their role in it, they slowly segregate themselves into a deep hole of despair feeling not quite good enough, for an unattainable utopia.

Perhaps religion or staying away from the seven deadly sins like pride and envy is a matter of keeping people healthy and happy. Perhaps the faceless dolls of the Amish give their children a space to dream in and truly become themselves in a way all the faces absorbed by media do not give other children. The Amish ability to separate these necessities and superficialities is helping to prevent them from being exposed to some of the modern plagues that technology has brought on our mental health including insecurities, bullying, lust, and so much more that is now just a click away.

It is odd to think that relationships always crumble over a lack of shared values and desires in the end. I was initially shocked in some sense to see that the Amish are more progressive and forward-thinking about sex than the 'English.' While it is not encouraged to have sex before marriage, it also isn't as shamed. It's in contrast to the culture I grew up in to think that my father was shamed more for having a car than for premarital sex. In the American mainstream culture, women are often shamed for sex, much more than their male counterparts. It calls to question all shaming when you look at a conservative culture that worries more about a car than sex versus an unconservative culture that puts a lot of shame on sex, particularly for women. Perhaps it is not the action that is the problem that causes shaming, but the people a culture wishes to control.

MORE STRUGGLES

The questions I asked as a child never left me. I looked for advice first from those whom I had known since I was young: my elders. Yet I got no answers. At about age thirteen, I decided I had to explore and find them on my own since no one in the community offered any. As I grew older, the experiences of my brothers and some of their friends only added to my curiosity and unrest.

When I was just entering my teens, my oldest brother Mose was drafted into the Vietnam War at age eighteen. Because the Amish don't believe in war, he requested stateside service as a conscientious objector and spent most of his two-year stint at the Mansfield General Hospital. He lived in Mansfield while he worked at the hospital and visited as often as possible, about every other weekend. Like a good Amish boy, he served his time and then returned as expected to Amish life and work.

My brother Eli was different. He was drafted when I was fifteen and served at Union Hospital in Dover with my cousin, Henry Mast. At the time Eli had an Amish girlfriend and was already a member of the church. By the end of their two years of service, both Eli and Henry had decided they wanted to leave the Amish life behind. They had bought a car together and announced they were going to stay in Dover.

The announcement did not go over well at home. The

boys' parents hatched a plan.

Datt, Memm, and Henry's parents went to Dover to talk to the boys. I never learned what transpired, but the boys' car was never seen again. Both boys came home late one night, escorted by their parents. I didn't even hear Eli climb into the bed next to mine.

The next morning Datt was waiting for me inside the house instead of out in the barn.

He said simply, "*Dah Eli ischt dehehm*" (Eli is home). He paused a long time before adding, "*Mahs ischt vie nix gehappened het*" (Just act like nothing happened).

My datt and I went to milk the cows in silence. Eli came down to breakfast, then headed out with us for the day's work. As Eli and I brushed the horses before harnessing them, Eli broke down in tears of frustration and rage.

"Brother, what's wrong?" I asked. Even though I knew the answer, I didn't know what else to say.

"I can't understand why they won't let me do what I want to do," he fumed as he walked away with one of the horses.

The Amish have a way of making people feel as though they have no options. The immutable dichotomy between staying Amish or being shunned and going to hell is a scary message for those who have never known any other life. Some people might consider that brainwashing, but I believe most Amish grow up actually believing in their ideals.

Many Amish never even read the Bible all the way through, so they have no real reason to believe anything different from what they have been taught. Some of the more rebellious Amish, even those who stayed in the community, may understand that life choices are not so black and white. I would be surprised if the Amish I know still truly believe that I am doomed to go to hell just because I no longer follow the Amish ways.

Eli got married shortly after his attempt to leave the community. In the end, he was glad he decided to stay in the fold, and later he even tried to help bring me back. Only many years later did I understand how Eli truly felt at the time and discovered firsthand how lonely it can be when your family is no longer a part of your life.

In 1969 my brother Jacob and our neighbor Henry Raber, who turned eighteen after the draft was eliminated, also decided they wanted to leave. Jacob told me about their plan shortly before they left. He said he would be in touch later but didn't want to give me any details so I wouldn't have to lie to Datt.

One Sunday morning someone came to our house and picked them up. They left without a word. Datt came right to me and asked what was going on.

"Jacob told me that he and Henry were leaving the Amish community. That's all they told me, though, Datt. I don't know where they went."

My datt spent several days pondering this information and then went over to Henry's father's house. Together the two of them managed to find out where the boys were staying. Together they convinced both boys to come back home. The next morning when I got up, Jacob was home again.

It was a challenge to be raised in an Amish home and attempt to go out into the world. We had virtually no knowledge of how the world worked outside the Amish community and rarely interacted with the English. We hadn't even graduated from high school. Leaving was a daunting challenge for an Amish person. Now, the communities interact a lot more with the English, but leaving is still difficult.

According to the deal Jacob made with my datt, he was allowed to have an outside job instead of working on the farm. He went on to marry his girlfriend, Esther, and join the church.

Jacob's experience taught me that if I wanted to leave, I had to stay home as long as possible, essentially until Datt threw me out of the house. That was the only way he would understand that it was truly my choice to leave. Regardless, he would try to bring me back, so I needed to know how to stay away if I wanted to. After watching two of my older brothers leave home only to come back, I knew when my turn came I had to plan my escape differently. The wheels in my brain started spinning, figuring out how I would arrange my exit from the community so I wouldn't be thwarted.

MY FIRST JOB

During the summer of my eighteenth birthday, now being legally able to make my own choices and decisions, I told my datt that I intended to pursue a path to get my religious questions answered. The idea was not to attempt an 'escape' the way my brothers had tried to do but to further my understanding of the Amish faith and lifestyle. I explained that the search might involve looking outside the community and that my first step in this process was to get a job, and later I would buy a car.

I told him, "Datt, I'm not going to abandon you mid-harvest. I'll stay through the harvest this year, but I won't be available next summer. I plan to have a job outside the farm by then. Still, I'll stay home as long as you need me to help with the chores."

My father nodded, but I don't think he believed I was serious.

It wasn't difficult for Amish people to get a job in the local community because they have a reputation for being responsible and hardworking. An Amish person was almost always hired over the average English worker without question.

My datt had taught me the adage: "If a job is once begun, never leave it until it is done. Be it labor great or small, do it well or not at all." I don't know if it's an Amish teaching or just something that he read and liked, but I have carried the advice with me my entire life and still follow it.

Several Amish people in my neighborhood already worked at Hipp Lumber, and I applied there in the fall of 1971 after the harvest was in. To my surprise, the company didn't require any information. They only gave me a short interview, then asked, "When can you start?"

"Whenever you want me to," I said.

"How about Monday?"

"Great!" And just like that, I had my first official job.

Traditionally, except for an allowance, Amish children turn all their money over to their parents until they are either twenty-one or married. So it came as no surprise to me when Datt asked for my first paycheck. He was dismayed by my response.

I said, "I told you my plan is to buy a car and search for answers to the question of why I should be Amish. That's why I won't turn my money over to you. But I'll make a deal with you—I'll give you half of every paycheck as long as you let me stay at home." And I faithfully gave my father fifty percent of my earnings from every paycheck, from the first one I received until he locked me out of the house. After that, I kept all my earnings.

Several Amish from my neighborhood were employed at Hipp Lumber, so transportation was by a group taxi. I started work at $1.70 an hour (minimum wage at the time) and thought I was making a lot of money! I was quite proud of my first job, earning more money in one hour than I had ever gotten for an allowance. Datt's allowances were sparse and only given when he was feeling kind-hearted.

———

Before I got the job at Hipp, my brothers and I had occasionally worked unofficially for a non-Amish neighbor, Owen Brenley. Owen and his wife had no kids, so we helped with their harvest and other projects around the farm. He was one of the few non-Amish people I felt close to. It took me some time running it over in my head, but finally, I got up the nerve to ask Owen the question that was on my mind.

"Um, Mr. Brenley. I'd like to talk to you about something."

"Sure, son, what is it?"

"Well, I have some questions about being Amish, and no one wants to answer them. I'm thinking about leaving the Amish community to find some answers. I know to do that, I'll need to learn a great deal. One of the more difficult things will be driving a car. Would you please teach me to drive?"

"Hmm, well, son, leaving the community is a pretty important decision. I think you should take a good while to think it over. I don't mind teaching you how to drive, but you must promise me one thing."

"Sure, what?"

"Your father can never, and I mean never, know I'm the one who taught you, OK? It would ruin our neighborly relationship."

"I promise I won't tell."

Our lessons started a few weeks later, first on his tractor. Owen's driving motto was "First the fields and then the roads." Once he felt comfortable with my skills in the field, he let me drive the tractor alone. Next, he taught me how to drive his truck, again first in the fields until finally, once I had my driver's permit, in his car on the street.

I knew no other way, so the system worked well for me.

In a few weeks, I felt confident enough to drive anywhere.

Owen also helped me find my first car, a 1962 Chevy. I saved my salary for two months before I had enough money for both car and insurance. It was listed for $150 but he helped me bargain it down to $125 (around $1,500 dollars today), and I finally bought it at the end of October 1971. The car had a dent in the front fender but was mechanically sound. Even though I didn't yet have my driver's license, just a permit, I was so proud!

THE CAR

"Datt, I bought a car, and I'm bringing it home tonight after work," I told my father.

"No," he said. "You can't stay here if you have a car."

"I know how you feel about cars. I won't bring it on the farm. I've already talked with Richard Slegal. He's agreed to let me keep it on his property. I'll walk home from there."

My datt bemoaned my decision but couldn't do anything about it. My mind was made up. I knew I couldn't keep the car on my datt's farm; in his mind, the car being on his land gave him the implied right to do what he wanted with it. I wasn't sure what he would do; I only knew I didn't have the money to fix or replace anything.

"How did you get your driver's license?" he asked.

"I have my permit, not a license yet."

Not long after this conversation, a friendly local sheriff's deputy approached me. Holmes County was a small community, where everyone knew everyone else. The officer said, "Son, you need to be careful. Your datt called and told us to keep an eye out for you. He gave us a description of your car along with the plate number and said you were driving without a license. We won't come looking for you, but if we find you driving without a licensed driver with you, we'll have to issue a citation. That would mean a fine and we would impound your car."

My datt's plan to get the sheriff to arrest me for driving backfired. Instead, he tipped me off to be extra cautious.

I did occasionally drive illegally, mostly to pick someone up so I could practice. But I was careful never to get caught and had a plan to get my license as soon as possible.

I went to the Department of Motor Vehicles with Henry Raber, thoroughly prepared for the test. Henry had left a neighboring Amish community, so he understood what I was going through.

I had been practicing driving with Owen and other friends for months, so on test day, I felt confident. I nailed the trickiest part of the exam—parallel parking—and was sure I would walk away with my license.

The instructor said, "Great job parking, and you did a good job driving. But you drove right through a school zone without slowing to the 25 MPH required by law. You have to watch the street signs. They're there for a reason. I'm sorry, but I have to fail you."

Crushed, I said, "Oh, I'm sorry, sir. I guess I was so focused I didn't notice the sign."

"It's OK, son. You can take the test again in a week's time," he said as he left.

Never one to give up, before even leaving the building I scheduled the next test seven days from my first test.

After the botched test, I re-drove the route with Henry Raber, paying careful attention to where the school zone was so I wouldn't make that mistake again.

Seven days later I walked out of the DMV with my driver's license. Datt was going to have to find another way to get rid of my car.

BROTHER JACOB'S WEDDING

Not long after I got my car, on November 16, 1971, my brother Jacob married our second cousin Esther. Since the Amish are such a close-knit community, marriage between second cousins is quite common. Just like in English society, among the Amish, marriage is not permitted for any relationship closer than a second cousin.

I was Jacob's equivalent to a best man. In the Amish tradition, both the bride and the groom choose a couple to witness for them as sort of a best man and maid of honor, called the nevahuka party.

The night before the wedding, all the nevahuckas went

to the house hosting the wedding to help prepare for the big day, like setting up benches. Now, most communities have a set of dishes that are carted around for big events, or use disposable dishes, but at the time, it was part of the nevahuckas' job to make sure everything was clean and sorted for the big day.

Dressed in our Sunday best—the same suit I regularly wore to church—we walked in with the bride and groom and sat next to them for the four-hour ceremony. Amish weddings are big, happy celebrations, similar to a church service in that they start at 8:30 AM with singing. Then Jacob and Esther left to talk to the preacher while everyone else continued to sing. Even though they had the required training on what to expect as husband and wife, this conversation reminded them of the significance of their journey to matrimony. When the bride and groom came back, they sat facing each other while the main preacher spoke, after which he read a scripture passage.

Finally, he turned to the couple. "If you still want to get married, come forward."

The preacher recited the marriage vows as Jacob and Esther repeated the words back to him. Then they returned to their seats and he said a final prayer. The service ended with more songs. The wedding had no personalized vows or big kiss; the point is for the couple to make their commitment to each other and God in front of the church community. The core principles of the Amish culture are what bind them together for health and happiness until death.

Jacob and Esther got a short break before meeting everyone for well-wishing at the reception. They sat at a table with the nevahuckas on either side of them for a family-style lunch.

The best part about Amish weddings is the food! Trays laden with mashed potatoes, noodles, applesauce, chicken, and other delicious homemade dishes were handed from table to table. Dessert was pudding, ice cream, and of course cake. Because the Amish work hard, they eat a lot, and the trays get passed around for second and third helpings.

Jacob's wedding was one of the last Amish events where I was accepted. At the time, I had already gained some status as a rebel, because I was working outside the farm and had just bought my car. It was made very clear to me before the wedding that I had to use a horse and buggy for this event, and that my car could not be seen. That was OK with me at the time. I was there to support my brother.

TAKING FLIGHT

Having a car was fun. It gave me some rebel status with my Rumspringa peers. While it isn't unheard of for Amish boys to buy cars during Rumspringa, the community always assumes that they will give up the car and come back to the church. Nowadays, it's even more common for Amish boys to have a car until they officially join the church. In my era that was rare, but still didn't make me a complete outsider.

I still ran around with my Amish friends. I often picked them up on Sunday afternoons and we drove around Millersburg, maybe stopping to get a burger or window shop.

One day two friends and I were out driving when we saw a sign advertising *AIRPLANE RIDES*. What teenage boy wouldn't think flying was a cool thing to do? None of us had ever been in an airplane. We went to investigate.

A middle-aged man wearing an American flag T-shirt and a John Deere hat looked up from the newspaper he was reading when we walked into the office. He must have been surprised to see three boys dressed in Amish garb at an airport.

"We saw the sign about airplane rides and want to know how much it costs."

"The three of youse want to go up?" he asked.

"Yes, sir."

"It's $15 per person for a 30-minute ride."

We pulled out our wallets and counted up our money. I had $18 and one of my friends had $15. The other friend didn't have the money, but he wasn't as excited about the ride as we were, so he waited on the ground. It was a lot of money for us and we barely had enough to cover it, but we would be in the clouds. What was money for if not to take a trip near heaven?

A few minutes later, a small four-seater plane roared to life with a pilot and two Amish boys, our faces glued to the windows. It was the thrill of a lifetime. I had never even imagined flying—nothing beneath me but air! The buildings looked like dollhouses and the cars like ants creeping along a ribbon of road. As the plane turned and dipped, it took me a few minutes to get over the sensation that I would fall out despite the sealed doors and windows. I heard the throb of the powerful engine and felt the speed and force of our movement, inside of falling we floated as if on water.

Orville and Wilber Wright might be the first brothers credited with flight in the US, but ours was another important historical flight that's been overlooked. We were most likely the first Amish whoever flew for pleasure.

As we left that day I made a promise to myself—I had learned to drive, and someday I would learn to fly.

THREATS

Once I had my driver's license, I used the car to get to work every day. One cold, snowy day when I just needed to stop at home and change my clothes, I didn't want to walk the half-mile from my usual parking spot. Instead, I parked by the buggy shed, right next to the house. My plan was to run into the house, change, and leave.

It was chore time and my datt was milking. As I turned the engine off he came running out. "You can't park here!" he yelled and immediately started to unscrew the air valves on my tires. It only took me a few seconds to realize that if he succeeded in letting the air out, I would be stranded, with no way to refill the tires. I quickly jumped back in and sped away, parking the car in its usual spot a half-mile from the house. I never tried to park near the house again.

Ever since I had gotten the car, my datt had repeatedly said, "You can't stay here." The tire episode was only one of many minor squabbles building up to a major dispute.

I had thought Datt had accepted me giving him half my paycheck. He never brought it up, even after I bought the car, until several months later. One day I came home from work and found him in my room, snooping around in my dresser drawers. He asked, "Where do you keep your money? You know it's mine."

"You didn't think I was dumb enough to leave it out where you could find it, did you? I keep it in my pocket, always with me, so you can't take it," I said solemnly.

To my utter surprise, he wrestled with me, trying to take my wallet from my pocket. Youth and desperation let me win this battle.

I said firmly, "We made a deal. You don't get to change that. I give you half of every paycheck, and the other half is my money."

My father wasn't a violent man. He just hoped that by taking my money, I couldn't keep the car. He knew money was tight for me, especially with our deal. Scraping together enough to buy the car had been a challenge to start with, and I had to pay for car insurance and gas. And to keep from standing out as Amish at work, I was saving to buy some English clothes. My hourly wage of $1.70 didn't go far, and I constantly counted pennies to make ends meet each month. At the same time, I was trying to save money for an apartment—I kept expecting Datt to kick me out of the house.

———

I still wrestled with the idea of what I wanted to do with my life. Hipp Lumber was a reasonably good job, but it didn't pay especially well. One day Gerald Hipp called me into his office.

He said, "We want you to know that you are doing a good job, and we are happy to have you work for us. But you should know your dad was here today and he wants me to fire you. He said he needs you at home." He paused and considered the look of shock on my face.

"Don't worry, I'm not firing you, nor would I, based on what your dad wants. But I do want you to think about it. If you want to go help your dad, that's OK. You don't even have to tell us. Just don't show up for work tomorrow, if you think that's best and what you want to do."

I didn't even have to think about it. "Sir, I appreciate you telling me this. I guess I shouldn't be surprised my dad would do that. He's tried almost everything else to get me to sell my car and stay home like a good Amish boy. But I have no intention of quitting my job. If I'm not fired, then I'll be here tomorrow."

This conversation made me think more and more about what I wanted out of my life and my future. I started to look for different options.

————

I wasn't the only one in our church district who had a car. About ten years before I bought mine, both Atlee and Mose Raber had cars. The Rabers let their sons live at home and park their cars on the farm during Rumspringa. Because owning a car was against Amish teachings, they suffered the consequences even though their sons were not yet members of the church. The parents were not allowed to take communion.

Atlee Raber also worked at Hipp Lumber. One day he asked me, "Hey, Albert, how is your datt handling you having a car?"

"I would say not very well. He called the police, hoping they'd arrest me for driving illegally, and even tried to get me fired. It could be better," I said.

Atlee said, "I probably shouldn't tell you this, but he came and talked to my datt and memm a while back when Mose and I were still at home. I assumed it was about church business. Afterward, my datt came and sat Mose and me down. He had to collect his thoughts before he told us, 'Samuel Miller came by tonight. He said the church wants us to kick you out and not let you come home unless you sell your cars and switch back to driving a horse and buggy. Now your memm and I have been put beside the church and are unwelcome for communion for as long as you both stay here with your cars.'

"I knew then that this was serious. The whole church must have discussed the question several times. And that's not all. Datt went on, 'Nothing would make your memm and me happier than if you sold your cars, drove a horse and buggy, and joined the church. But I would rather build a garage for your cars than ask you to leave. You just both need to know that we can't take communion as long as you are living here and own your cars.'

"I think my datt predicted what will happen to you in a few years, because he added, 'Samuel doesn't know what he's in for. Just wait until his boys get older.'"

Atlee paused, then said, "I'm so grateful my datt handled it like that. I'm just telling you about it so you're ready. I don't know if your datt will be different with you, or if he'll kick you out the way he asked my parents to do with us."

A twinge of jealousy swept over me. I wished I could have had a datt as understanding as Atlee's. I also realized that Atlee was trying to warn me that my datt might not back down in our conflicts, especially since he was the deacon of our church district. I needed a backup plan.

In the end, neither Mose nor Atlee Raber ever joined the Amish church. They both married English women. I sometimes wonder what it would have been like to be accepted for my different choices from the start. Perhaps I would have changed my mind and stayed Amish. But I wasn't, and I didn't.

PART 2
NEW HORIZONS

A LOCKED DOOR

Winter had arrived, and anyone who has driven in an Ohio winter knows the dangers of black ice. It lures drivers into thinking the roadway is clear and dry, encouraging them to accelerate just a bit before sending the car spinning wildly out of control. On one of those snowy winter days, I underestimated the ice monster. It took over the tires and I was ill-prepared to fight back. My beloved '62 Chevy slid off the road into a ditch, adding yet another dent to the ones I had already accumulated from posts and trees that seemed to pop out of nowhere every time I drove.

The dent itself wasn't the problem—a murky green fluid leaked into the snow as the car hissed like a rattlesnake. I had cracked the radiator.

A new radiator cost more than I had paid for the car. I sold it to the junkyard for parts, which barely covered the towing cost.

I couldn't afford to buy another car, but I needed to get to work. Until I saved enough money to buy another one, I rode the shared Amish taxi and started looking around for options. Eventually, I realized that either I would wait a long time to buy another car, or I had to borrow some money. Coworkers and friends suggested a local bank in the nearby town of Berlin, Ohio. I was already planning to open an account there when I had enough money saved. But I needed a loan now, and I had no idea how loans worked. I didn't know if it was even possible for me to get a loan. I did know that I didn't have either a checking or savings account and that no one would sign to guarantee the loan for me.

Nervously I sat down to talk to the man behind the humongous desk at the bank.

"How can I help ya, son?"

"Well, sir, I'd like to take out a loan for a car. My radiator broke and left me in a bit of a pinch."

"Do you have a job?"

"Yes, sir. I work at Hipp Lumber. I brought my pay stubs to show you."

"And do you have an account with us?"

"No sir, not yet."

"Just a minute then, and let me see what we can do for you." He took my papers and walked into a back room. I took a deep breath as he came back.

"Well, Mr. Albert Miller, it looks like we can give you a loan of up to $500 dollars. To do that, you need to fill out this paperwork. Pay close attention to the 4 percent interest charge here. The bank will hold title to the car until you pay off the loan. And you need to open a checking or savings account with us."

"How will I get license plates then?"

"Don't worry, you'll have all the documentation you need to handle that once the paperwork is complete. Payments of $65 are due once a month."

I walked out of the bank with a checking account and $450 dollars in cash. My next stop was Stutzman Motors, where I found a black Mercury for $525. I had saved $100 dollars toward my apartment and put part of that toward the car. Yet again, I was one step further from moving into an apartment, but at least I had a car again.

When I got home that night with my new car, my datt didn't waste a minute.

"This accident is a sign from God, Albert, that He doesn't want you to have a car. Don't keep repeating the same mistakes."

I didn't think the accident was a sign from God. What frustrated me most was the further delay in getting an apartment. Even with overtime my paychecks never reached $100, hovering around $80 a week. I needed money for insurance and other car expenses, so my savings, between the bank and my pocket, had dwindled to just $50 until my next paycheck—not near ready for me to commit to an apartment.

One Sunday evening in mid-January, when the cold air stung exposed skin like tiny needles, the wind cut right through my clothes, and the snow was piling up quickly, my datt's threats finally materialized. I parked my car in my usual spot and walked the half-mile home as quickly as I could, trying not to inhale the painfully frigid air.

Like every other night, I pulled on the door handle. It didn't budge. At first thinking it was stuck with the cold, I yanked harder.

Then I heard the clink as the lock pin met the metal casing. The door was locked. Not once in my life had I seen one of our doors locked. I had never seen a key to our doors, didn't even know where to look for a key if I thought one might be kept around.

I had not heeded Atlee Raber's warning, and it had caught up with me. The cold seemed to fade away—something I consciously knew was still there but could no longer feel—as I tried to think. Confusion washed over me as I contemplated my next move. I saw a soft light pulse from behind the door. A flashlight. Through the glass, I could see the outline of my mother and father on the other side of the door. They were up and had been waiting in the dark for me to come home.

"Albert?" Muffled by the door, my datt's voice sounded unusually unsure.

"Yes," I said, shivering.

"I've told you over and over again that you can't stay here if you keep that car of yours," he said, his voice more authoritative now.

The wind carried my defiance through the keyhole. "And I told you I'm keeping the car."

"Well, you need to sell the car if you want to stay here."

Cold and bone-tired, I replied, "Can't I just stay here a bit longer until I find a place to stay?"

"Sell the car, Albert."

"What about if I stay just tonight?" The cold whipped down the porch and sliced through all my layers. If only all my clothes weren't still in the house.

"You can't have a car and stay under my roof."

I contemplated the ultimatum. I knew my father was

stubborn. This back-and-forth game through the door wouldn't end unless I gave in. If I stayed out here for hours, his response would be the same, and I knew it. I caved.

"Fine, I'll sell my car."

The key turned in the lock and the door opened. I closed the door behind me and felt the warmth start to soak in at last. We stood for a few moments in silence, staring at each other. In the dim circle of the flashlight, my parents looked older than I remembered from the morning. Finally, I broke the silence.

"Before you say thank you or anything, I'm sorry. I lied to you just now. But I need to go upstairs and get my clothes and things before I leave."

My father and mother looked at me with pain and disappointment written all over their faces. My father merely nodded at me. I started up the stairs but turned back. "I will understand if you don't want me to, but could you let me sleep here just one more night? I have nowhere to go right now, and it's very late to be asking someone if I can sleep at their house."

In fact, I had lined up the house of an ex-Amish friend who worked with me, ready for just such an occasion, but my parents didn't know that. Andy Yoder and Henry Raber had promised me a couch if I needed it. However, nearly midnight is not a respectable time to call on someone for a favor unless you have no other options. I figured I had nothing to lose by asking my parents. They wanted me out of the house, but maybe I could get one more night.

My parents looked at each other. Then my father said, "Albert, you can stay here tonight, but we will not bend the rules a single night more. If you come back again with the car, there is no extension."

"I understand, Datt. Tomorrow I'll get up and go to work, as usual, then I'll come home to get my things and then be out of your hair."

It was hard to sleep that night even though I was out of the cold. My mind raced from idea to idea, making plans for my new life.

How will I carry my things?

An Amish home has nothing like bags or suitcases.

After an unrestful night's sleep and a distracted day at work, I came back to my childhood home for the last time. My family was eating supper without me. I went up to my room and wrapped as many of my pants, shirts, long johns, and underwear together as I could into a bundle. I had nothing besides my Amish clothing and couldn't afford any new clothes. I carried as much as I could and left the rest. Laden with my belongings wrapped up and tied in a shirt with a knot, I had to walk past my family again to leave. I paused for a moment, looking at them. I felt like I should say something, but wasn't sure what that something should be.

"Where will you go?" one of my siblings asked.

"I don't know right now. I don't have an apartment yet, so I'll stay with some friends until I can afford my own place."

I was intentionally vague because I didn't want them to know where I was going. "I'll let you know when I have a permanent place to stay."

"Well, write when you do," my father said without looking up from his plate.

Then Memm and my younger siblings Mary, Anna, Susy, Esther, Ella, and John focused on their plates again. I turned my back on them and headed out into the unknown.

As I drove away, I remembered how Jacob and Eli had wanted to leave and were coerced into coming back home again.

Should I write or not? Letters would only let my parents know where I was, and I had no doubt they would come and try to convince me to go back. I wasn't sure I could handle the pressure or whether I would cave as my brothers had, so I decided not to write. I didn't write a single letter until after they found me, three months later.

I stayed with Henry and Andy until I found an apartment in Berlin, sleeping on their couch while I saved my money. I hadn't known that renting an apartment required a deposit of one month's rent upfront in addition to the monthly rent. Who would have thought?

I saved every penny I could and only spent money on essentials: food, gas, and car insurance. By March I felt like the king of a castle in my $90-a-month apartment. It was a tiny one-bedroom, not much to look at and with no furniture, but it was mine. I couldn't afford even a mattress and slept on the floor. After the first week, I stopped by the local Salvation Army, where I found a discounted couch. I slept on that for several weeks.

My meals were limited and as cheap as possible to save

for other needs and to ensure I could make the rent each month. Three meals a day on a monthly food budget of only $40 was a struggle. Cereal served for any time of day, usually Cheerios or corn flakes. I ate hot dogs on bread or peanut butter and jelly sandwiches.

New clothing didn't make the cut, so I continued to wear my Amish clothes although I knew they made me stand out. The road to somewhere new is narrow, and along the way, life weaves as much into the past as out of it.

THE VISIT

By the time April peeked through the ashy bleakness of the Ohio winter, I had added two chairs and a small table to my couch and mattress. One cold Ohio day dreary with a misty rain just shy of snow, my doorbell rang. I was surprised and puzzled. I hadn't made a lot of new friends and didn't expect anyone from the Amish community to visit me. I opened my front door and found my father and my brother, Eli.

"Eh, hi," I squeaked, in shock.

"Hi there, Albert," my brother said, staring at me with a sad face. I wondered if it had been his idea to come or if my datt had made him. He seemed more like hired muscle than a real participant in the conversation that followed. Does he truly believe what our datt is saying, or not? But clearly, this was not the best time to have that conversation.

"How did you find where I live?" I asked.

My datt said, "Come on, Albert, we have our ways. You know that. Now, we need you to come home. You've had your fun and your time away. It's time to act like you're supposed to. You don't need to worry about the car or the apartment." He waved his hand dismissively at the door. "I'll have someone take care of all that for you."

I opened the door a bit more. "Please, come in and we can talk about it."

"Albert, we will not support this lifestyle. We will not come in."

The rain was white noise, like a radio that wouldn't stay tuned in, as we stood in the doorway.

"Your little brother John cries every night for you to come home. And we pray for you every day."

The guilt twisted my stomach into knots, but I kept my resolve. "Datt, I am staying here."

For almost an hour, he listed reason after reason for me to come home. I held my ground and refused to break, but the guilt got heavy and tiresome. Finally, I'd had enough.

"It's awfully chilly and I'm cold. I am not coming home, Datt. I want answers, and I couldn't get them from you. I need to do this alone. If God wants me to be Amish once I find these answers, then I'll come home. But until then I will follow the journey He is leading me on. If you want to come in out of the cold and talk, you are welcome here. But I won't keep standing out here in the rain and cold."

I went back inside and they stood frozen outside my door.

"I'm going to close the door if you don't come in." Still, they stood, looking at me.

"Come home sometime to visit," Eli finally said.

"Sure, I will," I said, still in shock. I closed the door and slumped onto the couch, emotionally drained.

———

Even though I had a job and my own apartment, I hadn't left everything behind. I continued to hang out with my Amish friends and see my Amish girlfriend. We had been dating pretty seriously for about a year before I left. I had told her then that I didn't want to be Amish and asked if she would leave with me.

The conversation had been uncomfortable, to say the least. Initially, I thought she seemed interested and was willing to leave with me. Looking back now, I heard what I wanted to hear. She wasn't nearly as excited about the prospect of leaving as I was. Even though we had talked at length about leaving and our plans, reality hit and she had second thoughts once I actually left home.

One time I visited her, her datt came to speak with me.

"Albert, just sell the car and go back to live with your memm and datt," he said.

I said, "I can't do that, sir. I have questions about God and the Bible and need to find the answers." With that I left, not wanting to cause a problem between my girlfriend and her datt.

But the exchange made me question our relationship. The more she and I talked, the clearer it became that she didn't want to leave the Amish community and that my car was becoming a bigger and bigger issue.

In the end, we broke up. We wanted different things out of life.

STRAINED TIES

After Datt and Eli found my apartment, I started going home for visits. I wanted to try to have some reasonable contact with my family. I didn't have many other friends and, honestly, I felt lonely and lost. I knew I needed to explore and learn on my own, but I missed the community and the people. In Amish society, a person is rarely alone. There are always people around you who you can depend on. In the outside world, I had learned, that people kept more to themselves.

I went home every two or three weeks, but the visits didn't make me feel any less lonely. The warm welcome I dreamed of simply didn't exist.

"Oh, you thought of us," said my mother.

"Oh, it's you," was the most my father could muster.

Never a *Hello* or *How are you?* They showed no interest in my life, except to ask three questions:

"Where do you live?"

"Where do you work?"

"Are you married?"

They never asked anything else, just spent the rest of the time talking about Amish things. Those three questions seemed to be all they wanted to know about my life for the next ten years.

Even my siblings had banded together to encourage me to come back home so I could officially be welcomed back into the fold. The strategy only made me feel like an alien.

Every now and then I received a letter from someone, inviting me home for a special occasion, generally a Saturday or Sunday, which were typical visiting days. The letter would say, "The others are coming too," which meant my married siblings. On these occasions they let me eat a meal and play games like ping-pong, almost like old times.

On these visits, my datt always tried to convince me to come home, one way or another. I missed my family, but I knew I would only come home once I understood the *why* of my questions.

One day, I asked my datt and one of the younger preachers of the church to talk with me. I wanted them to explain why I should be Amish, and have an honest and open discussion. I needed to make a decision based on understanding. But my datt merely said that wasn't an option. He refused to even entertain the idea of an open dialogue.

I wanted to understand the reason for how I had been treated, and why I should be Amish. Yet my datt denied even these requests to help me understand. He believed in simply following the rules.

"Albert, just do as you are told," he growled. I think he was embarrassed to even consider bringing other people from the church, especially a preacher, to witness his shame: my choice to leave.

The rest of my family seemed most concerned about my soul.

"Albert, without God you won't go to heaven," one sister said.

"I can't believe how terrible you're being to Memm and Datt. Don't you know how much you're hurting them?" another sibling chimed in.

"Grow up! Haven't you had enough fun yet?"

"Don't you think you've proven your point?"

"What even is the point you're trying to prove?"

"You know in the end you'll come back. Just stop making everyone suffer."

"I just hope you figure it out before it's too late and you end up in hell."

————

On one of my visits Datt said before I left, "*Duh verscht bessa op vahn duh gestaubasht vahn duh graunk vaust vie ein babee.*" (You would have been better off if you died when you were sick as a baby.) "At least then I know you would have gone to heaven because you were innocent. Now with these wild ways of yours, I fear for your soul and that you will go directly to hell."

His words hit me like a punch to the gut.

My father was not someone to mince words. He was an

honest man who taught me to be honest, truthful, and to work hard. He believed in straight talk and simple justice. I tried to imagine how he meant these words, considering his very literal ideas, but mostly they just stung.

My father's life was lived with clear examples of integrity and honesty that never left me. Once he had bought a boar from a neighbor. He used the boar for breeding that season and then sold it. Datt had paid the neighbor $100 but sold the boar for $120. Even though it had been months since he purchased the boar, he went directly to our neighbor and shared the $20 profit in a fair split, $10 each, as if that was the natural thing for someone to do.

For as much as I hated him sometimes for his harsh words, my father was a good man. I knew that deep down he thought he was doing what was right, even if perhaps it wasn't, and he might later regret it.

These lectures of his went on for the next few years, and I tried to remind myself that he thought he was doing what was right. That wasn't always easy to do, considering that I was still working to define for myself what was right.

———

On one visit home I made an announcement about what I anticipated to be the start of a deeply spiritual journey. I thought perhaps it would help ease my family's worries about my soul—and my return home.

"I am not anti-God. I want to understand Him for myself. So I have bought a Bible to study in German and English so I can understand its teachings. The High German version is complicated to read, and I think I can understand it better in English." Blank stares and silence greeted my great announcement.

By this time I had visited most of the churches in my area: Catholic, Mennonite, Methodist, Lutheran, and the rest. All of them felt they were right. *How could that be? Are they all right? Maybe it doesn't matter.*

I couldn't convince my father to sit down with me and discuss biblical issues to help me understand why I should be Amish. I felt it was time to share my resolution with my family.

"I have decided to read from page one to the last page of the Bible, instead of being confused by the selected verses that each religion chooses to focus on. I want to find in the Bible, for myself, what it is that God wants me to do. I also promised myself I would accomplish this in a year. If at the end I find a reason in the Bible why I should be Amish, I will sell my car and return home to live an Amish life."

My sister, Esther, was the first to speak. "Why do you want to read the Bible in English? The Bible was written in German."

The question caught me off-guard. I thought that she should have known the truth.

"I know your Bible is in German, but that's because you speak Pennsylvania Dutch. The original Bible wasn't written in German or English, but in Latin or Hebrew, and then translated." I knew the Bible had been written in an ancient language and honestly didn't know which one, but I refused to reveal my ignorance at that important moment.

My datt was a respectable man who read a lot, and he confirmed my response. "You're right, Albert. It was originally written in Hebrew, then translated into Latin and then into all the other languages."

That was the end of the conversation.

A DAUGHTER'S REALIZATION

Here my dad chimed in to show me just how smart my grandpa was, "He knew when you moved to Brazil that it is on the other side of the equator and the seasons were different. He found it fascinating!"

I was kind of amazed that he had even cared. I always had the distinct impression that my grandpa didn't think much of me, especially because I was a girl. He was always much more interested in talking to my brother, even though I played all the same sports as my brother. It had always bothered me to be overlooked as a girl, mostly because as a child I felt that all the time. I was a pretty intense tomboy who everyone kept trying to ply with pink items, dresses, sewing, and cooking lessons. It was very discouraging for me to feel like my love of the color blue, and getting dirty, and sports meant I couldn't be a girl 'enough' for anyone. I learned to just ignore their ideas and go about doing my own thing.

So to think that my grandpa was finally impressed

with something I chose to do made me wonder what other bits of him I missed out on having pigeon-holed him into this narrow viewpoint. Everyone has something unique to share, whether you agree with their general viewpoints or not.

After I turned twenty-one, my father again raised the question of money on one of my visits home to see the family. This time he took a new approach.

"Albert, you know all that money you earned and kept, you really owe us. I want to know how and when you intend to pay it all back." I guess I shouldn't have been surprised, but he caught me off guard.

After a few minutes, I replied, "For me, it would be easier if you adjust your will to even it out." I thought that seemed to be a fair and appropriate response. Even so, his reply was exactly what I expected to hear.

"Albert, you know our beliefs. So you know with the way you've behaved you won't even be in our will. Don't expect a penny from us."

"That is your right. But of course, legally I don't owe you anything either. Since the day I turned eighteen, I have had the right to keep all the money I earn. Besides, I contributed a good deal of free labor for you all the years I worked on the farm."

He dropped the topic after that.

———

While I so often found it difficult to go home to be around my family because of how they treated me, at times I was proud of them. These times somehow stand out more in my memory than the negative ones.

In 1972 I was still unsure who was my friend and who was my foe. One day I stopped by my brother Mose's farm to visit. Almost no one in my family would talk to me by then, especially Datt. I knew that even just visiting could cause problems for Mose, but I missed him.

My visit caught him during milking hours, so we chatted as he milked. His oldest son, Ivan, was just old enough to be walking around and was curious. He stood nearby, quietly watching us. A noise outside the barn caught my attention and I stepped outside the barn to make sure my car was OK. I heard Ivan take the opportunity to ask my brother, "Datt, vehr ischt sela mann?" (Dad, who is that man?) I waited, curious how my brother would answer.

Mose looked at his son and said, "Sel ischt dah Albaht. Her iz mya brutta ischt vie dah Sam dia brutta ischt" (Well, that is Albert. He's my brother, same as Sam is your brother.) "He's just not Amish anymore and lives up in Berlin. He came to visit us today." Then he went back to milking as Ivan looked at me curiously.

I was proud of how my brother had answered the question. It was nice for once to not feel like an outsider. I felt accepted at that moment, something I didn't feel often anymore in my childhood community.

IN BETWEEN

It's awkward and uncomfortable being stuck in the in-between. Not quite in, not quite out; not quite sure who I was or where I belonged. I think everyone feels this way at some point in their lives, but for me, this in-between time was a stark divide between being Amish and being English.

Learning to navigate my new world was not easy. With each turn, I glanced over my shoulder, longing for the sense of safety, community, and home the Amish had once been for me. Yet an impenetrable wall separated that life from my current one.

For the first few years, after I moved to Berlin, I worked at the lumber mill before getting a job at a cheese factory. My job at Guggisberg Cheese Factory paid more than minimum wage, but not by much. I worked in a number of different roles. The morning started with the intake of milk, delivered almost exclusively from local Amish farmers. Milk in cans could not be sold as Grade A for drinking but was used to make Guggisberg baby Swiss cheese, which was well known in the area.

My initial job was to test each can to make sure the milk wasn't sour—not always a particularly appetizing job! Spoiling mostly occurred during the summer, since the Amish didn't use refrigeration, especially the Saturday evening milk that had been held for pickup until Monday. If the milk had soured, it was my responsibility to return those cans to the owners.

Since I was the only licensed driver who worked in the cheese house, on the rare occasions that one of the truck drivers couldn't drive the route, I was the backup. Sometimes I had to pick up milk in my old neighborhood. Thankfully, I never had to go to my datt's house, but several people in my old district were on the route. Sometimes they greeted me kindly, but mostly they ignored me. One thing I was sure of, they gossiped about my new job.

My datt came to see Mr. Guggisberg to express his displeasure that I was working there. He threatened Mr. Guggisberg's business, saying that if I was driving his milk truck then the Amish would not send their milk with me.

Mr. Guggisberg had a temper. When he tracked me down in the storeroom later that day, he was red in the face. I knew he was angry; I just wasn't sure why.

"Look here, Albert, I don't know what is going on between you and your father. But he came to talk to me today. That man thinks he can get his own way by threatening me. I mean, the nerve of him! If anyone says anything to you about not giving you their milk because your father wants you to quit, you don't say anything. You just get back in the truck and drive away. Leave their milk behind. I don't care if their milk sours; it'll serve them right." With that, he stomped back to his office and slammed the door. I had never seen my datt make someone so angry before.

No one ever refused to give me milk on the few occasions I drove the route. However, knowing that my datt had tried yet again to get me fired made me once again consider other career options.

What could I do long-term?

Would I want to work in a store?

What about cleaning carpets?

I spent a lot of time thinking, not so much acting on my thoughts. I was raised to think for myself and work hard; I just wasn't sure how to go about life in the English world. I did feel that someday I wanted to have my own business and work for myself, but how? I needed a gentle push in the right direction, or I'd end up stuck in the land of indecision.

At Guggisberg I met an Amish man who did plumbing and electrical work, which seemed strange since he didn't have any electricity in his own house. Since I got off early from the cheese factory, I started to be his chauffeur. Members from my church district would never have ridden with me, but he did because he was from a different district and didn't need to shun me. It was convenient for him to have someone who spoke Pennsylvania Dutch. After a while, he also hired me to help with the plumbing and some of the electrical work. Trying new jobs was a great way for me to learn skills and explore different careers.

I was looking for a long-term career that would support a family if and when I got married. College was never a consideration for me.

In the back of my mind, I knew I could return to the simple Amish life, although it was far from what I wanted. Nor did I feel it was what God was leading me to do. I kept it as my backup option, knowing that if I was willing to sell the car and start wearing my Amish clothing again, the community would welcome me back. Based on my reading of the Bible, I had given up the belief that the dress code and lifestyle were necessary. I believed I was saved by the blood of Jesus.

I needed to consider my path if I didn't return to the community.

What could I do with my life?

Should I open my own business?

How do I make a life for myself, alone, in an America that I am still learning to navigate?

How can I be sure that it will be a life I can be proud of?

Will I still foster the will of God if I choose to set my own path?

NO LONGER AMISH

My brother-in-law Mose, Anna's husband, and I were buddies long before he started dating my sister. We had run around together during Rumspringa and stayed close. I didn't imagine he felt any different about me once I started questioning my Amish roots because things between us seemed to be the same. I thought the rest of the Amish community also saw me as the same Amish boy I had always been, but I learned all too quickly that was not true.

Although I had my apartment, I still went to Amish

events. My cousin Ben's wedding, on April 27, 1972, was right next to my former Amish girlfriend's house. It was practically a family reunion. Even though I hadn't been personally invited, each Amish family typically gets only one invitation. Since I wasn't living with my family, I hadn't seen the invitation, but assumed I was included. Family and friends of friends are always welcome since the Amish community relies so much on each other.

At the wedding celebration, I mingled with family and friends for a while. At first, I didn't initially notice the shift in climate, but there must have been some discussion among the wedding party and the people hosting the wedding. Two guys, the ushers who organized the horses and buggies as people entered, blocked my entrance to the wedding seating.

"You are not welcome here," one of them said.

I tried to explain. "Look, I don't want any trouble. I'm just here for the wedding. I still respect the community; I'm just exploring options and taking this year to read the Bible."

They weren't interested in hearing what I had to say.

"Go on, back outside. You aren't welcome."

"But why?" I said, once again searching for answers.

It was clear they weren't going to let me stay, and I was pushing my luck. They walked me out to my car, even as I tried to talk my way back into the wedding. I thought we were having a healthy conversation and never saw what came next. I guess they felt I was being too aggressive.

WHACK! The strike from the flashlight sent me reeling

backward against my car.

The buggies and horses blurred. I don't know what shocked me more—the searing pain, or the sudden violence of someone I considered a friend.

OK, maybe not a good friend, but aren't we all one community?

The message was clear. I was no longer a part of the community.

I groped for my car door, blood trickling down my cheek. I sat, dazed, as other guests pulled up unaware. My assailant walked back toward the house, unconcerned.

I started the car and drove to Joel Pomerene Hospital. The doctor put five stitches in my scalp, but the pain of that exclusion took years to recede.

I had already stopped seeing my Amish girlfriend because the difference in our choices was clear. It hadn't dawned on me until that moment that I might have to stop seeing everyone.

I needed to make a decision.

Did I want to be part of my Amish friends' lives?

Did I need to cut them out of my life?

Had they already cut me out of theirs?

Did I want to be associated with a group of people who no longer wanted anything to do with me?

That night I decided I was no longer Amish. The community obviously didn't want me around anymore, and I would not be a part of a group of people who treated me with hostility. I stopped attending Rumspringa singings, weddings, and other reunions. I didn't attend another Amish event until years later after I was married.

––––––––

I continued my personal journey to read the Bible from beginning to end. If I was no longer wanted among the Amish, I needed to find a place where I would be welcomed. I continued to explore and visit non-Amish churches. Most importantly, I joined the Holmes County Post High Youth Group and started to make new non-Amish friends.

I came to the conclusion that the Bible does not teach that we must follow certain dogmas or doctrines to have a ticket to heaven. Rather, it teaches that the grace of Jesus Christ is what matters. I began to define the religion that I would choose to follow: one that emphasized a personal relationship with God and Jesus.

At the end of my biblical search year, I wanted to explain my findings to my family. I had read from page one of Genesis to the last page of Revelation without skipping a verse. After that, I suddenly wondered, *What am I going to do now?*

I realized I had to make a long-term decision: *Would I be Amish or not?*

If I decided not to be, I knew I had a lot to learn. I had to learn how to function in the non-Amish community and date non-Amish women. I was utterly on my own.

A few weeks later I planned to officially tell my parents I wouldn't be coming back home to live with them. I was proud to be able to tell them I felt that I had a good relationship with God and Jesus. I firmly believed that, Amish or not, I was on my way to heaven.

It was a much bigger deal for me to share my religious journey than it was for my family to hear the news. Despite my sense that they had already given up on me by the time I was ready to reveal my explorations, eagerly I gathered them together.

"I've read the whole Bible cover to cover. I can see in many parts where the Amish get their views from, things like the separation of church and wearing head coverings. If you read only parts of the Bible, being Amish makes sense.

"But if you read the whole Bible, you get a different view than from just reading verses here or there. For example, Paul's letters were written for a specific purpose. They say, 'Go into the world and witness.' But nowhere does it say you can't have a car or a phone or electricity.

"I will follow the letters of Paul and go into the world. I have decided to join a Mennonite church in Berlin."

I had picked this church specifically because in many ways Mennonite beliefs were comparable to the Amish religion, and I hoped my family would be more accepting of it. I explained the many similarities between the two churches.

No one had much to say, nor did anyone seem shocked. I didn't know whether my family had already written me off, or if they had just gotten used to not having me around.

———

On subsequent visits, my family seemed to have given up on even trying to talk me into coming back into the Amish fold. The visits were always the same. I was greeted with the same unenthusiastic distaste and the same bland questions.

"Oh, you thought of us again."

"Where do you live?"

"Where do you work?"

"Are you married?"

"This lifestyle of yours will lead you straight to hell, Albert."

Their comments always stressed how my life was evil and I was destined for hell. My visits quickly became tiresome.

I started to wonder if this cycle would persist my whole life. No matter what I did, my exploration of faith and life outside the community disappointed my family. They treated me as an outsider. I was lonely.

Would I never have a family?

Would I always be on the fringes?

I knew I had to stop thinking about what I had left behind and start thinking about what I wanted out of my new life. It was time to pay attention to things like dating English women, my career, and my future.

How do I date an English woman?

How will I make a living long term?

Do I want to get married?

What kind of a career do I want?

How do I do any of these things in the English world?

SHUNNING

If I had known at the time I was going to be treated the way I was when I left, I am not sure I ever would have done it.

My whole life had been in the Amish community, and suddenly I was shunned. Everything familiar was taken away; I had nowhere to go, no one to turn to. It felt like I had moved to another country, one where I knew most of the language and almost none of the culture. I had to start over to learn the lifestyle and try my best to fit in. I had to learn to speak English more fluently and needed guidance in even simple English cultural ways. It has turned out to be a life-long learning experience.

This culture shock is in part why shunning is still such a powerful tool among the Amish. Those who consider leaving never get to see the perks of living in the English world; they see only the shunning—the stark absence of friends and family, the loneliness. These negative aspects often deter many Amish from even questioning their options. Not everyone, whether they feel the impulse or not, has the constitution to leave everything they know behind and venture into the unknown, even if the unknown is right next door. That is why everything the Amish need to know for the future is taught in a one-room schoolhouse.

There is a loneliness unique to shunning, a deep disconnection. Even a lonely English person knows other people and can reach out to connect with them. When I was shunned, I was cut off, left to struggle alone. Every attempt I made to connect only pushed me farther and farther down—like someone holding my head underwater until I gave in so they could let me up to breathe.

My father had done everything in his power to convince me to come back home: asked, threatened, called the police, tried to get me fired from my job. When those failed, he enforced the cold shoulder. I was no longer welcome at family events. Many church members looked away when I passed, refusing even to greet me. The contrast from the warmth and love I once knew from the community left a dark void.

Only one person sent me a message:

Albert,

Please stop by to visit us. We know you are being treated unfairly.
In faith,

John Yoder and family

At the time I thought about going to visit them. It felt good to have that message of support, but I didn't want them to get in trouble with the church. I feared that if word got out that I had visited them, they would suffer the consequences.

Even my own family refused to greet me. Every attempt

I made to maintain a relationship with them meant that I heard I was going to hell. Hearing nothing but the crushing weight of others' judgment, without a foundation to even give it merit, quickly became a burden too difficult to bear.

Now I enjoy traveling and going to different countries, and although the languages are challenging, I often find more disparity in the Amish and American cultures than I find between the American culture and those of Mexico or Brazil. Learning English-American life was more difficult and challenging than any foreign culture I have encountered. I stepped out into 'English-America,' as a native-born American, to find myself in this so-called land of dreams - to find the American within me.

A DAUGHTER'S DIVERGENCE

If little material things can separate a community and people of faith, how can they not be materialistic? Perhaps since I attended only one Amish church service as a child I can't speak much to the Amish faith, but what little I saw of the community seemed more on par with treating each other with love than malice. Though shunning others for not believing the same thing or stressing over the number of buttons doesn't make sense to me.

For me, it has always been hard to imagine a 'divine being' who seemed so selective about whom to give love to. Withholding love or knowledge based on something as superficial as gender, sexual preference, or a car never made sense to me. The line between roles, choices, and personal freedoms is a murky one when religion comes into the mix. I can't help but wonder if religions led with a more compassionate feminine touch might not help everyone feel a bit closer to a loving God instead of an ambivalent one.

Considering I live far from my family, I can't help but notice some similarities between my dad and me. I also often feel a bit outside, nothing like being shunned, but perhaps the farther you move from what others know, the more on the fringes you stay. Though in the end, I am not sure I would trade all my life experiences just to be off the fringes and more in the circle.

It is hard for me to make it home for all the events, and my reality is so different at times, that it can be hard to think of relevant conversation. I miss key cultural events and pop culture references. I forget how to say things in English or am unaware of how basic services work in a country I almost never use them in, even if it is my country of birth.

Sometimes my siblings don't seem interested in my life, since I chose something 'other'. It's hard for me to know how much of my 'otherness' is based on my choices versus just differences in personality and values. Perhaps I would face all of this if I was in the same county, but being farther away makes the void seem greater.

Perhaps it is always the path of the other, 'the black

sheep,' the oddball, to go out and feel never quite as connected as we wish in exchange for something new or different. In the end, the irony of it all is that we can never be sure what we missed as compared to what we gained. So when we choose our 'path less taken' we must do so with the conviction of being right — because to have been wrong would hurt too much.

HOLMES COUNTY POST HIGH

I needed to find a new community, one that would support my choices. One of the most supportive groups for me at the time was the Holmes County Post High Group, a Christian youth group for those who had graduated from high school. They held a number of events together, from Bible studies to bonfires, and the group was an easy way to meet people. The community was very welcoming and open, which helped since I still didn't understand English life, much less adjusted to it.

John Schmidt, a gifted musician, and guitarist, Eli Hochstetler, better known as "Small," and Ernie Hershberger were three people from this community that had a great influence on my life.

Small, a former Amish member as well, was the person I identified with most. He helped me grasp the difference between the Christian belief of being saved by grace compared to the Amish tenet of being saved by works. He was the person who most changed my spiritual life by showing me the Christian faith that I still follow today. He was my guiding light on this new journey of beginnings.

Ernie Hershberger, was a pivotal force in my life, the one who challenged me to go to college. I am forever indebted to him. Without him encouraging me to pursue further education, my life would not be what it is today.

This group was the new crew that I ran around with. They helped me adjust to English life by explaining aspects that confused me and supporting me in this new and bewildering world. It was with their encouragement that I started my path toward a future away from the Amish community.

For one of our first adventures, they took me to visit Pittsburgh, Pennsylvania. I was twenty years old and had never left Ohio. I was so excited, expecting big things, sure that a new state was a whole new world. I was bitterly disappointed when we crossed the state line and I realized Pennsylvania was no different from Ohio.

I could hardly distinguish the two. If I hadn't seen the *Welcome to Pennsylvania* sign, I wouldn't have even known I had gone to another state. I felt lied to. Not that anyone had told me it would be different; I just assumed it would be. It was the first of many times when I learned that my own assumptions often led to my greatest disappointments.

———

The Holmes County Post High group held its last meeting for the season early in the fall, before most of the members returned to college. I was twenty-one years old and still uncertain about what I wanted to do with my life. After the meeting, Ernie sat down next to me and started to talk.

"Bert, how's it make you feel to see these other youth group kids going off to college?"

"I don't know." I shrugged. "I'll miss them, but I know they'll be back around." I honestly hadn't really considered it before.

"What would you do if you could do anything you wanted?"

"But I can't do anything I want."

"Come on now, Bert, let's just imagine you could. What would it be?"

"But Ernie, I never went to high school. There is no way I can do whatever I want."

Ernie, being persistent, said, "Well, let's just imagine that you did finish high school and the whole world was open to you. Now, what would you do?"

"I'd be a dentist."

"Well then, why don't you?"

"I can't."

"What do you mean you can't? What are you doing tomorrow?"

"I don't have any plans yet." I wondered how I could become a dentist tomorrow.

"Great! Tomorrow we are going to talk to Mr. Finn, the

Highland High School principal. I think you could take the GED test and make that dream of being a dentist come true."

"What's a GED?"

Ernie explained that the GED was a test to certify high school-level equivalency skills. He said he would pick me up the next morning at my house at eight o'clock.

Mr. Finn was tall and slender with glasses and dark hair. He had that principal air of importance. He asked me a lot of questions.

"How were you in math?"

"Pretty good. I used to get As."

"What about English?"

"Good. I got As and Bs, but only in the first five grades. The Amish parochial school I went to in 6th, 7th, and 8th grade didn't include English."

"How about spelling?"

"Pretty much the same as English."

"Did you like school and studying?"

"Sure. It was always my favorite part of the day. Excuse me, Mr. Finn, is there some kind of a prep course for taking the GED?" I asked.

"Honestly, it seems like you are a bright boy. The test is mostly just reading a section of text and then answering questions about it. Plus it sounds like the math part won't be a problem for you, so I don't really think you need a prep course. I think you should just read a book or an article in a newspaper, and when you are done with it reflect on what you learned from the story. Then come up with some questions that you would ask someone about the story. That's essentially what the GED test will be like."

I followed Mr. Finn's advice—reading, reflecting, and developing questions as my study course for the GED. I was a bit skeptical that was all I would need, but I went on faith. I had always loved school. I could have kept studying forever if someone had paid me to attend. It wasn't until after I quit being Amish and started to study again that I realized how much I enjoyed it.

On the assigned day, I arrived at the school. The test was held in a small room with maybe ten other people. I felt intimidated since I had never taken any kind of standardized test.

There was no timeframe for completion; I could take as long as I needed. The test included a math section, with the rest of it reading passages about social studies, history, and similar topics, followed by simple questions. Basically, the test evaluated whether I could comprehend what I read and if I knew some basic math and English. The whole thing took me three or four hours and was easier than I had imagined.

The results came in the mail a few weeks later. I felt as though I'd won a ticket to the future when I saw that I had passed all areas of the test. Now I could really dream about the future!

What does the future hold for me? Maybe college?

What would that cost? How would I pay for it?

Would I even be accepted? Would I be able to study and pass the classes?

Would I fail? What if I got in, spent all that money, and then failed?

PART 3

A THIRST FOR LEARNING

KENT STATE

Kent State is a state-supported public university. At that time public universities and colleges were required to accept everyone who passed the GED for at least one semester at the school.

However, it was not a "no strings attached" deal. First, I had to meet with an intake counselor. Then the school gave me a series of pretests to ensure I could keep up with the material before I was allowed to enroll. My intake counselor was Joan Miller, who was a psychology teacher at the school. She was only a little older than me: young, calm, and quiet-spoken. She administered the entrance exams and talked with me about my goals. I told her I wanted to be a dentist.

Since I only had a GED, I met with Joan a number of times for a series of assessments. One of the assessments noted that I read very slowly, only about thirty words a minute. Instead of writing me off as a failure, Joan put me in contact with an optometrist friend who worked specifically with children to help them learn to read more efficiently and effectively. I think she didn't have much hope of me passing college classes at the time, but she knew if I was going to make it through school I needed to read faster, or I wouldn't be able to keep up with my studies. Everyone seemed to think I would fail.

Joan was very kind and patient. She looked over my scores and asked if I had thought about a vocational school—not the first time I had heard this suggestion. The vocational school was just across the street from Kent State's local branch campus, and I reassured Joan that it was my backup plan. Despite her doubts about my abilities, she maintained her positive and supportive attitude.

I finally passed enough entrance exams to get into Kent State—barely. Joan gave me a tour of the campus and showed me how to find her office. She said she was there for me if I ever needed to discuss anything. I registered that day for my first two years at Kent on their Tuscarawas branch campus, signing up for English, political science, math, and biology.

––––––––

The first time I saw the reading specialist eye doctor in Dover, I was twenty-one and just starting college. I took classes from him to learn how to keep my eyes flowing across the page and read continuously. He taught me strategies to ensure that I wasn't just reading the words but also absorbing the content.

"Pay the most attention to the first and last sentence of each paragraph. Then stop and think in your head about what you have read. Repeat it back to me when you are ready," he said.

After much practice, I didn't need to stop as long between paragraphs. Then I didn't need to stop at all. These classes were essential in helping me learn to read faster and comprehend better.

More importantly, this doctor also diagnosed me with

amblyopia, a lazy eye, in my right eye. I wondered how an eye could be lazy.

Perhaps it just wasn't as strong as the other eye?

Can I make it stronger?

With his guidance, I learned that a lazy eye at my age was a problem that could not be fixed. It meant my depth perception is not as good as other people's. If the lazy eye had been addressed when I was young, my vision might have normalized as an adult. Children with lazy eyes often wear an eye patch to train their eyes. If their vision is really bad, doctors can perform muscle surgery. Unfortunately, once children reach their teens a lazy eye is not really treatable. It was too late to fix my eye now. My eyes had already learned not to focus together and were set in their ways.

As the doctor explained lazy eye and what it meant for me, his words suddenly put into context something I had long forgotten. When I was in public school, we had mandatory tests on both our eyes and ears. My teacher repeatedly sent me home with notes stating that I needed to see an eye doctor. When I showed them to my parents, my datt asked, "Can you see the blackboard to read it?"

"Sure I can," I said. As a child, I had only ever seen one way. How could I know there was a better way to see?

My memm said, "If you can see the blackboard and read, then you don't need to see an eye doctor."

Turns out my parents were wrong. While I'm not completely blind in my right eye; my brain basically ignores information processed by that eye other than for peripheral

YOU CAN'T DO THAT!

vision. On the optometrist's eye charts, I can see the first rows of letters and that is it. The other lines run together into a solid line.

A DAUGHTER'S VISION

Vision is a tricky thing because we assume everyone sees the same when that is not the case. People see colors differently or not at all and have different vision strengths. How do we ever know if we are seeing anything the same as anyone else?

Like my dad, I too understood the struggle of never realizing things for other people were different. From the most basic lack of good vision: when in third grade, I excitedly stared out the window as we drove off with my new glasses.

"Mom! The trees are 3-D!" I exclaimed. Because up to that point I had seen everything as a blurred backdrop and never known that the rest of the world didn't see things the same.

But, it was also a visionary shock in life to realize that my childhood was in many ways not 'normal.' Not only because I had divorced parents in a time when divorced parents weren't the norm, nor because my father had grown up Amish and all my relatives on that side were Amish, but more because of the unique experience of being raised by a mother who was ill in many senses of the word. Growing up with a mother who had psychological issues meant that it took me until I was almost a teenager to work out that her ideas of punishments, and norms for dealing with situations, were by no means a normal reaction nor healthy, but that experience in itself is a tale for another story.

For my dad, gaining his sight must have been more challenging: not just his physical vision which he never got 100%, but also trying to see clearly in his new life. He needed to gain the ability to see through what was different both culturally and for him as an individual.

Kent State was on a far different level from my elementary school and the GED test. I finally understood why people had been concerned before I started.

Math was harder than before, but still the easiest of the four classes I took. I had trouble with all of them but got a third of the way into the semester before I felt the first real wave of distress.

On the first day of class, my English teacher had given us a quiz on grammar and punctuation rules, with concepts like prepositions and conjunctions. I didn't have a clue what the words conjunction and prepositional phrase even meant. I sort of understood pronouns, but English was the hardest of my courses. By a third of the way through the semester, I had done a couple of English quizzes and was completely discouraged: I was getting Cs.

With a defeated feeling and a somewhat sad face, I walked into Ms. Miller's office. She looked up at me with a friendly smile and seemed happy to see me.

"I wanted to thank you for giving me the opportunity to try here at the university. But I think I need to quit. This isn't for me. I would like information on vocational school if you still have it."

"Sit down, Albert, let's talk about this. Honestly, I expected to see you much sooner. How are you doing?"

"I'm getting a *C* in English, and maybe a *B* in math," I said, dejected.

Joan was all positive. "You're passing? If you're getting *C*s, you can't quit now. Imagine how much better you'll do next semester! Do you know where you are compared to your classmates?"

"Honestly, I hadn't considered that. I'm just used to getting *A*s and *B*s."

"I can arrange some intermediate classes and tutors to help you. Please just promise me that you will wait until the end of the semester before you decide whether or not to quit. I think you are doing great, all things considered."

"I guess I could stick it out, with a bit more help." Joan had roused my spirits.

That first semester I got a *C* in English but eked out Bs in all my other classes. After that first semester, I never saw another *C*.

From then on, Joan was not just my counselor. She became a friend, advisor, and confidant. I went to see her frequently. We talked not only about school but also about coping with my rejection from the Amish community. As a psychologist, she helped me deal with all my life struggles. Her support and encouragement were invaluable in working through moments of doubt. She never gave me specific direction on what to do, merely asked questions and made observations. Her comments helped me clarify my thinking and understand who I wanted to become as a person.

"You have choices on how you handle your life, and your parents have choices on how they handle their life. In fact, they have the right to treat you any way they choose. They have chosen to treat you in a negative way, and it is their right to do so. It may not feel good, but once you give them that right, you will feel better."

Ultimately, support from Joan gave me the courage to speak my mind to my parents. At the time I still made trips home every few weeks, but the conversations were always the same:

"Oh, you thought of us again."

"Where do you live?"

"Where do you work?"

"Are you married?"

And the conversations went downhill from there, always devolving into shaming that only made me feel worse and worse.

The most thought-provoking, hurtful, and difficult thing my datt ever said on one of my visits home was,

"Es ischt tsoo fiel. Ich kahns ischt baud nicht mahha vahn sie mich finna vie dah Jonas es ischt deine schult." (It's just too much. Albert, I'm just so disappointed in you. Your choice has

made life very difficult for me. If they find me like Jonas Yoder [the bishop who committed suicide], it will be your fault.)

Hearing your father threaten suicide and blame it on you is difficult. However, my conversations with Joan gave me the courage to respond to these comments with a cool head. Advice from another non-Amish friend also helped keep my emotions in check. My friend had told me to never make rash decisions—always stop and think of three things to say, and then pick the best of the three before responding.

So when my datt talked about suicide, I finally had the strength and courage to pause and think before replying. "Datt, I understand that I have been a disappointment and have upset you. I want you to understand, though, that I made those choices of my own free will, and I believe they are the right choices for me. I accept full responsibility for them. But I will not accept responsibility for your choices. Those are on you."

I did not have a fun drive home that night, even though I felt confident in my response. The threat of suicide was the meanest ploy I'd heard my datt try. That night I prayed that nothing bad would happen to him and that God would give both me and my father the strength to do the right thing. I thought of that conversation frequently, worrying that my datt would take his own life, which he never did.

I continued to visit my parents regularly, hoping to have my parents see me as a good kid even though I was not Amish and was different from them. Finally, I got to the point where reality set in: I felt a relationship between us was never going to happen. Having done all I could to bolster the connection between us, I felt I was forcing a relationship that was no longer possible. When I realized this, our relationship simply ceased to be a priority to me anymore. I decided on my next visit I would bring this up with them.

"I have tried as hard as I can to maintain a relationship with you, but I don't see you making a similar effort. My sense is that you aren't interested in having any relationship. From this point on I won't be coming home as frequently. I will still visit from time to time, but not as often."

Secretly I hoped that something would change. Maybe the threat of losing me would mean I could get back part of that sense of family I missed.

My memm said, "Well, Albert, what do you expect us to do?"

"I don't expect to be treated like my siblings who are still Amish, but I hope you could treat me like your non-Amish neighbors, like Ralph Kaser and Roy Conkle. I guess the least I expect is a friendly greeting when I come home. A simple 'hello' would suffice."

My parents shrugged off my concerns.

That friendly greeting didn't happen on my next visit, so my visits home dwindled to once every six to twelve months. The energy I had been focusing on my family I invested instead into growing my own life and making new friends. Without my Amish family, I created my own adopted family.

I wouldn't hear from my parents for six months or more if

I didn't make an effort to see them. Then I would get a letter from Memm or Datt, and if I didn't respond they'd send a letter every week until I wrote back. They just wanted to know I was alive, and once I understood that I sent letters back as often as possible.

———

I maintained a full-time job while at school, working at Union Hospital as an orderly to see if I liked working with people. This was the same hospital where my brother Eli had worked during his draft service. Many of the staff remembered him and gave me a warm reception.

At Union Hospital, I met Mike Sluetz, another orderly, who became one of my closest friends. We were like brothers throughout my university days. Mike and his wife, Kathy, helped me assimilate to the English culture, particularly helping me learn to dress like the English.

When I was Amish, I usually wore a white or maybe a light blue shirt with blue pants. It was easy. The English world offered a whole rainbow of colors, including the currently fashionable plaids and stripes. Mike and Kathy told me I needed to match. So I bought red-and-white checkered pants and paired them with a red-and-white striped shirt. Kathy and Mike kindly told me that subtlety was a better choice—perhaps a plain white shirt went better with checkered pants. Slowly my style adjusted, but even now I still ask for help from my wife.

I liked my job. There I met Dr. Kenneth Van Epps,

whose wife had Amish roots, and we became friends. He was fascinated by my journey from an Amish farm boy to a university student. He also served as my mentor, letting me shadow him in his office to get a clear understanding of his job. His mentorship sparked my interest in becoming a doctor, and I soon changed my major to pre-med.

With this new goal, I majored in psychology, adding a minor in biology with a pre-med focus. And I started to make contacts with doctors to learn more about their work. The mentorship of Dr. Van Epps and his twin brother, Keith, both doctors at Union Hospital, led me to drop dentistry altogether, though I knew getting into medical school would be a challenge. Kent State later offered me a place in their psychology Ph.D. program. They were rooting for me to get into medical school, but knowing I had a backup plan took some of the pressure off.

———

In my third year, I moved to Kent's main campus. Because holding a full-time job was the only way I could afford school, I found a new job at Robinson Memorial Hospital as an orderly and later became a respiratory therapist. I was one of the few employees selected to receive on-the-job training in this new position, which put me in more direct-care contact with patients. I began to see medicine's potential for my future.

BROTHER JOHN

While I was at Kent State, my brother John turned sixteen and entered Rumspringa. He wanted to see me, so I arranged to pick him up and have him spend a Saturday night at my place. I showed him what I was doing at both the university and my job.

John was very curious about my different way of life. He was trying to decide for himself what he wanted to do.

"You know, little brother, there's nothing wrong with being Amish. Many wonderful things revolve around the Amish community. It just wasn't the path for me. I had to choose a different course," I said.

"But don't you worry about going to heaven?" he asked.

"I have studied the Bible at length, and yes, I know I am doing things differently from the Amish. Yet I firmly believe that I will get into heaven." I explained to him that my church worships and believes in the same God as the Amish church, though it stresses the belief in being saved by grace, not what clothes I wear or what I do.

We talked a lot about religion and my new beliefs and discussed everything I had left behind. I explained how leaving had not been easy and that there were many things I missed.

I told him about my plans to finish my degree at Kent State and pursue medical school. I knew how difficult it would be to get into medical school and stressed the importance of having a backup plan.

"Everything comes with a price. No matter what you choose to do, I want you to know I will support you. If you want to leave the Amish, I'll help you any way I can. But if you just want to buy a car and be rebellious, then I want no part of that. I don't think you should do that just to be a rebel. I won't help you cause strife in the family."

John never got a car and he stayed Amish. Still, he was my closest contact in the family, and we have stayed in touch throughout the years. He serves as my go-between for other family members and is always the one who calls to inform me about invitations home, family issues, illnesses, and deaths.

I was no longer invited to reunions or weddings but was always told about funerals. I would go to close relatives' funerals to pay my respects. Funerals were the limited contact I had with the Amish community at large. I suppose death makes people realize that much of life's strife is trivial when we face the great unknown.

THE MEDICAL SCHOOL CHALLENGE

To be honest, no one thinks about their trusted doctor not graduating high school. A GED isn't typically considered a reputable background for academic success. However, I had worked hard at Kent State to maintain my grades and always had a job to help cover school costs. My dream now was to go to medical school and become a doctor.

Kent State, Akron University, and Youngstown University had a combined medical school called Northeast Ohio Universities, College of Medicine (NEOUCOM). I took some research assistantships there to make contacts and form a network. I also studied for the MCAT, the test required for applications to medical school. Joan Miller, along with my new friendly professors at NEOUCOM, coached me on how to handle medical interviews and what to do if I got a rejection letter. They said not to give up with a rejection letter alone, and to call instead and request an interview. Their help and support made me feel ready to apply. I was lucky to have so many supportive people on my side.

I applied to six Ohio schools: Case Western, Wright State, the University of Cincinnati, Ohio State, NEOUCOM, and the University of Toledo. Plus I sent one application to a private, non-state funded school, as oftentimes they look at unique candidates differently; Bowman-Grey in North Carolina was my only out-of-state application. Each application was diligently filled out by hand and mailed away. Sending the applications felt like sending a wish out and hoping it returned with my dream. The waiting was the worst part. I just handed the decision over to God and prayed that it was the right step.

I applied early decision to the University of Cincinnati because it was my first choice. Not only did it have a great medical school, but it was also the most affordable. I was barely paying off the costs of Kent State at the time and already knew I would need loans for medical school.

Since the University of Cincinnati was an early-decision application, it was the first response I got back.

When a manila envelope from Cincinnati arrived in my mail, I could tell there were papers in it. However, I had no idea whether it was the weight of acceptance or the lightness of denial. I stared at the envelope for a while before gathering the courage to open it.

I pulled out the paper and began to read:

```
Dear Mr Miller :

Your  medical  school  application  has  been
reviewed  on  an  individual  basis  and  also
comparatively  with  the  several  thousand
applications we have received for our limited
192 places in the next entering class. After
careful consideration of all aspects of your
application,  the  Committee  has  decided  to
discontinue  further  consideration  of  your
request for admission.

Therefore, your record has been moved to our
inactive files.

Please be assured that this decision is based
on our process and should not be construed as
a  reflection  on  your  general  suitability  for
medical studies.

I  am  sorry  that  it  is  impossible  to
communicate this information to you in a more
personalized manner; however, the exceedingly
large application pool precludes this.
```

Thank you for your interest in our Medical College and we wish you every success in your commitment to a career in medicine.
Sincerely,

Walter F. Leavell, M.D.
Chairman, Admissions Committee

The one great and positive lesson I learned from leaving the Amish community was to not be afraid to try things. Losing everything is a continuous life lesson in courage.

My application had been denied. Instead of wallowing in despair, I decided to be proactive. Realizing this step might be needed, Joan and I had discussed the possibility and planned a response to an application denial. Ready to try an unconventional approach, I rehearsed in my head the phone conversation I wanted to have with the dean who had signed my letter. Taking a deep breath, I picked up the telephone and dialed the number. Then I sat down at the table with my letter in front of me, serious and prepared for the conversation.

"Hello, I'd like to speak with Dr. Walter Leavell, please... Regarding an application for Albert Miller to medical school... Sure, I can hold."

In the end, I didn't talk to Dr. Leavell. Instead, the receptionist connected me to someone in charge of minority admission applications. I didn't understand why I was being transferred, but at least I had the chance to talk to someone.

After what seemed like a long silence, a voice from the other end of the phone line came on with; "How may I help you?"

My nervous response was as follows.

"Hello. This is Albert Miller. First, I want to thank the university for their quick response to my early-decision application to the University of Cincinnati College of Medicine. However, I am obviously disappointed about the decision. Considering my Amish background and where I have come from, I don't think I can be appropriately evaluated based on the standard paperwork. I'm calling to ask if you would consider giving me an interview. I think an interview would provide a much better basis for an adequate evaluation than just paperwork . . . Of course, if after the interview you don't think I'm a good candidate for your program, then I will respect your decision. But I think, considering my unusual circumstances, an interview is a better assessment of where I have come from and where I plan to go. I think I have done quite well with the tools I have been given."

There was a long pause on the line. I held my breath. *Had I spoken too long?* I worried that maybe the line had cut off and I hadn't noticed. Out of nerves, I talked almost non-stop. *Was he even listening?*

"Well, Albert, I do see here that you have some unusual circumstances. We will review your application further. I need to confer with some of my colleagues. Please call us back next week."

"Thank you very much, sir. I appreciate your consideration. I'll call you back in a week's time."

That was the longest week of my life. But the day before I was set to call back, I got another letter from the university.

```
Dear Mr. Miller:

As a result of your request, your AMCAS
application has been re-evaluated. There
is agreement to give it full evaluation and
therefore it will be returned to active status.
We will be pleased to receive the rest of
your application materials. I regret that I am
unable to be enthusiastic about the ultimate
outcome.
Sincerely,

Robert T. Binhammer, Ph.D.
Associate Dean
Secretary, Committee on Admissions
```

I called back to see what information the university needed me to submit with my application. Once I got together all the reference letters and additional material, I sent my dream off for a second time.

This time weeks passed before I heard back. Then another manila envelope arrived.

Dear Mr. Miller:

I am happy to tell you that your application has been reviewed, and that the Committee on Admissions now asks that you come to Cincinnati for an interview. Because your visit to the College will include meeting with a member of the Admissions Committee and a tour of the facilities, we suggest you plan on spending at least two hours with us.

Please call the Admissions Office at (513) XXX-XXXX to arrange a time that is mutually convenient.

I'm looking forward to meeting you soon.

Sincerely yours,

Norma E. Wagoner, Ph.D.
Associate Dean Co-Chairperson,
Committee on Admissions

I dialed the number and waited.

"Hello."

"Hi, this is Albert Miller. I received a letter to call about scheduling an interview for medical school."

"Oh, Albert, yes, wonderful. I have a note right here about you. Does next Friday at 10 AM at the College of Medicine work for you?"

"Yes, that works well."

"Please come directly to the admissions office and they

will direct you accordingly."

"Thank you very much. I will be there."

And just like that my rejection became a second chance.

Right away I started to practice for my interview. Joan helped me rehearse. The best advice she gave was to not answer questions right away but to pause and think about my response before answering. A well-thought-out reply is always better than rushing just to say something.

I also asked friends and some people I worked with to coach me. One of my biology professors advised me on what types of questions to expect.

My biggest worry before the interview was what to wear. My fashion sense hadn't advanced much since my days in the Amish community, and the only suit I owned was my Amish one. I managed to put together a presentable outfit— my best white dress shirt with a borrowed blue sports coat and tie, paired with some pressed gray slacks.

I drove down to Cincinnati for what ended up being a very long day. It wasn't just one interview, as I had anticipated, but multiple interviews with different people. After two individual interviews, I met with a group of people. That interview took almost all day!

At one point one of the faculty asked me a question I still remember: "Let's just assume that we accept you into the program. And now you've graduated and are Dr. Miller. Let's say you are working as a doctor, and something happens— one of your patients dies as a result of something you did or something you neglected to do. How would you feel?"

This was not an easy question. Fortunately, my interview training kicked in.

I bought a bit of time to think by saying, "Well, honestly I wasn't expecting that question. Let me think for a moment." I paused, then picked the best of the three answers I had come up with.

"Naturally, I would be devastated. But I also realize that it might happen. I sincerely hope that it won't happen in my first year, my first five years, or my first decade of practice. I fully understand it might happen in the future, and if it did happen I hope I would have enough of a background by then that I could focus on the people I saved, people whose lives are now better because of my help, instead of letting one instance cloud all the good work I did. I would hope to learn from the error, and never have it happen again."

Such questions are the reality of the medical field, although people don't like to think about them. At the time I couldn't tell if the interviewers approved of my answer and wondered what they had expected me to say.

Later in my career, I had to go to court for a case, and the experience reminded me of this question. A child died of meningitis after being seen by the pediatrician, who failed to catch the infection. I saw the child in the emergency room the next day, making me the secondary doctor. However, the original pediatrician should have diagnosed the disease. By the time I saw the patient in the emergency room, the infection had been too overwhelming and there was little I could do. It was already too late.

Everyone agreed that I was not at fault. Even the plaintiff's attorneys agreed, but the plaintiff still managed to bargain for $75,000 to finance the suit against the pediatrician and clinic involved. Sometimes, though, justice doesn't always come from the law. And no amount of money won in a lawsuit could ever bring back the parents' lost child.

The medical school interview was a grueling ordeal. At the end, I shook the interviewers' hands and thanked them for the opportunity. They in turn thanked me for coming. As I drove home, I honestly felt that I had done the best I could possibly do and had to leave the decision in God's hands. I had shown my merits, and if that was enough I would get in. However, I knew it was also possible that they had already decided my background wasn't sufficient, in which case nothing I could do would get me in. I was content with my chance to highlight my qualities and felt I had gotten a fair process for my application.

About three weeks later, another envelope arrived in the mail from the University of Cincinnati Medical School Admissions Office. It was just a regular letter; the small size of the envelope looked disappointing.

I brought the letter inside and paced around, too nervous to open it. I wasn't sure I was ready to handle a final rejection.

No one else was there to cry or cheer with me. It took me a while to muster the courage to open that envelope all by myself. My biggest fear was not being rejected, but having to tell everyone who had supported me that I had failed.

If Cincinnati won't take me, can I interview at other schools?

Will I have to beg for interviews with them too?

Finally, I got up the nerve to open the letter.

```
Dear Albert Miller:

Congratulations...
```

At just the sight of that one word, I cried. I didn't even read the rest of the letter right away. Tears of relief, joy, and accomplishment streamed down my face as I slumped to the floor, too emotional to stand.

```
Dear Mr. Miller:

Congratulations! The Committee on Admissions
of the University of Cincinnati College of
Medicine is pleased to offer you admission
to the entering class of September 1979. We
congratulate you on your achievement leading
to the selection for admission, and it is our
hope that you will accept this offer.
   In order to hold a place in the entering class
of 1979 you need not make a deposit. However,
you must indicate, in writing, your acceptance
by February 1, 1979.
   If we have not heard from you by that date,
we will assume that you do not wish to accept
the offer.
   Please understand that our offer for admission
```

is contingent upon successful completion of your current curriculum as well as the courses required in the catalog of the Medical College.

You should also be aware that the medical college offers a deferred admissions plan. Students requesting deferral of enrollment will have a guaranteed place in the September 1980 entering class; however, you are not obligated to enroll. A letter requesting deferral is all that is needed. Requests must be made prior to July 1, 1979.

Do not hesitate to ask us any questions you may have concerning admission both now or later in the year. May we also suggest that you notify and thank those persons who have given you active assistance during the long process of admission, for they deserve such a courtesy and will find comfort in your success.

Again, we hope you will choose to be with us next September.

Sincerely yours,

Walter F. Leavell, M.D.
Chairman, Committee on Admissions

When I finally read the whole letter, the first person I called was my best friend, Mike. His family lived near Cincinnati, so he offered his family's place to stay while I looked for an apartment, if I needed it.

Then I called and shared the happy news with my community—the friends, neighbors, and professors who had helped me prepare, practice, and achieve acceptance. Next to myself, the person most thrilled by the news was Joan Miller, who had helped me every step of the way. Everyone was overjoyed to hear my excitement and reveled in my accomplishment.

Because they didn't have a phone, my parents and siblings couldn't share in my excitement. In fact, considering the state of our relationship, I'm certain the news would only have saddened them. That no longer mattered to me, now that I had created my own supportive English family.

Next, I sat down at the table to write my letter of acceptance.

Dear Sir:

This letter is to inform you that I am pleased to have been offered a position in the September 1979 entering class by the Admissions Committee, and I appreciatively accept this position.

I am looking forward to being with you next September

I now will be seeking to obtain monies in the form of grants, scholarships, or loans to finance my education. Any information that you can offer on programs available through the College of Medicine or outside financial aid will be greatly appreciated.

Sincerely,

Albert Miller

I wrote another five letters to the other schools where I had applied, thanking them for the opportunity to apply and explaining that I had accepted a position at a different school.

Medical school was in my future. My interview had secured me a spot; it certainly wasn't my application alone. Once more my perseverance in the face of adversity had presented me with a new and exciting challenge to undertake.

INTO THE BIG CITY

Acceptance to medical school sent me over the moon. Somehow a local paper got wind of the news, and I got a call from Peggy Rader requesting an interview. I was shocked that anyone would want to interview me.

She wanted to write an article for the *Akron Beacon Journal* about the local Amish boy who was going to medical school. Their profile would describe my journey from Amish to university graduate on his way to medical school. I was pretty proud of myself, so I agreed to do the story.

To add interest to the story, Peggy and I drove to Holmes County and took a picture of me in my Amish clothes in front of the Green Ridge one-room schoolhouse where I completed my eighth-grade education. (The left half of this book cover is a reproduction of this photo.) Then we went back to Kent State University and shot the second picture of me dressed in English clothes in front of the school's student center.

The *Akron Beacon Journal* ran both photos on the cover with the caption, "Fresh from a one-room Amish schoolhouse, Bert Miller made it through Kent State—and now he's shooting to become a doctor. His folks are plenty mad." I didn't much like the last sentence. I hadn't said it and was sure my parents hadn't been interviewed. I always thought my parents were more sad than mad. But I didn't get to approve the article before it went to press, and I had limited input. I was disappointed about that. It was more negative than I wanted it to be toward the Amish.

Different med student

Banished by Amish Family, He Hopes to be Doctor

COLUMBUS, Ohio (AP) -- Albert Miller used to wonder, as a child growing up in an Amish community in rural Coshocton County, why his parents could not have a car like other families.

When he left home at age 18 to work at a lumber mill, Miller took this wonderment with him. It got him into trouble with his family.

Miller used his income from the job to buy a battered old car, something that was unforgivable among his strict Old Amish sect, which shuns modern conveniences.

Miller's father, a deacon in the church, barred his son's return to the family home unless he promised to get rid of the car.

"In essence, I was kicked out." he said.

Miller had only the $125 car and the clothes on his back, so he agreed to his father's demands. But when his parents let him in, he took back his word and, carrying an armload of clothes, left home for good.

As a result, he has for all practical purposes been banished by his family.

Tuesday, May 22, 1979   The Repository   23

Different med student

Banished by Amish family, he hopes to be doctor

COLUMBUS, Ohio (AP) — Albert Miller used to wonder, as a child growing up in an Amish community in rural Coshocton county, why his parents could not have a car like other families.

When he left home at age 16 to work at a lumber mill, Miller took this wonderment with him. It got him into trouble with his family.

Miller used his income from the job to buy a battered old car, something that was unforgivable among his strict Old Amish sect, which shuns modern conveniences.

Miller's father, a deacon in the church, barred his son's return to the family home unless he promised to get rid of the car.

"In essence, I was kicked out," he said. Miller had only the $125 car and the clothes on his back, so he agreed to his father's demands. But when his parents let him in, he took back his word and, carrying an armload of clothes, left home for good.

As a result, he has for all practical purposes been banished by his family.

Miller turned his back, he said, on a farming life it would have meant marrying a nice Amish girl, moving in with her family or close to his own, and sometime between the ages of 16 and 20, joining the Amish church, something he did not do.

The fifth of 11 children, Miller possessed only an eighth grade education then. He had attended public school through the fifth grade, and a one-room Amish school the last three years where "the basics of English, arithmetic and some Amish history were taught."

When he fled from the family farm in 1972, he did not know who was president and had never heard of the Vietnam War. Newspapers, radios and television sets were not available in the Miller household.

Miller went to work at a local cheese factory where he took in milk, primarily from Amish farms.

He had thoughts about going to school once more, but felt that his slight education ruled out college. Still, when he began working as an orderly for the Union Hospital in Dover, he investigated the branch campus of Kent State University at nearby New Philadelphia.

Miller took a test to make up for his lack of a high school diploma, and enrolled at the Kent State branch. As a freshman, he was introduced "to such things as negative numbers" for the first time.

To pay for the education he received $1,800 in student loans, and earned the rest working as a hospital orderly and for an ambulance company at the same time, and later as respiratory care technician. Still, financial problems caused him to drop out of school the first quarter of what would have been his senior year.

Miller, now 25, continued striving for a career in medicine, however. He is now completing his degree at Kent, and will begin classes next fall at the University of Cincinnati College of Medicine.

Getting into medical school proved a challenge. Miller applied to and was rejected by nine schools, including Cincinnati. His acceptance to Cincinnati came only after more testing and additional consideration.

And along with the acceptance came new problems. Miller's outside work as a medical student will be limited, he said, and without cooperation from his parents, obtaining financial assistance is difficult.

Miller turned his back, he said, on a farming life. It would have meant marrying a nice Amish girl, moving in with her family or close to his own, and sometime between the ages of 16 and 20, joining the Amish church, something he did not do.

The fifth of 11 children, Miller possessed only an eighth-grade education then. He had attended public school through the fifth grade, and a one-room Amish school the last three years where "the basics of English, arithmetic, and some Amish history were taught."

When he fled from the family farm in 1972, he did not know who was president and had never heard of the Vietnam War. Newspapers, radios, and television sets were not available in the Miller household.

Miller went to work at a local cheese factory where he took in milk, primarily from Amish farms.

He had thoughts about going to school once more, but felt that his slight education ruled out college. Still, when he began working as an orderly for the Union Hospital in Dover, he investigated the branch campus of Kent State University at nearby New Philadelphia.

Miller took a test to make up for his lack of a high school diploma, and enrolled at the Kent State branch. As a freshman, he was introduced "to such things as negative numbers" for the first time.

To pay for the education he received $1,800 in school loans, and earned the rest working as a hospital orderly and for an ambulance company at the same time, and later as a respiratory-care technician. Still, financial problems caused him to drop out of school the first quarter of what would have been his senior year. Miller, now 25, continued striving for a career in medicine, however. He is now completing his degree at Kent, and will begin classes next fall at the University of Cincinnati College of Medicine.

Getting into medical school proved a challenge. Miller applied to and was rejected by nine schools, including Cincinnati. His acceptance to Cincinnati came only after more testing and additional consideration.

And along with the acceptance came new problems. Miller's outside work as a medical student will be limited, he said, and without cooperation from his parents, obtaining financial assistance is difficult.

The story was picked up by the Associated Press and parts of it were reprinted across the nation, including in the *Cincinnati Enquirer*. A number of people wrote letters in response—some from old friends or colleagues and others from total strangers sending positive wishes or words of encouragement.

By far the most impactful letter was from Dr. Don Nofziger, a pediatrician, and his wife, Ann. They wrote to me saying they had read the article and as Mennonites were excited to meet me, offering to help me assimilate in any way I needed. I wrote back to thank them and tell them I would let them know when I got to Cincinnati.

Unusual college student

Ex-Amishman is finishing at KSU, now plans to attend medical school

COLUMBUS (AP) — Albert Miller used to wonder, as a child growing up in an Amish community in rural Coshocton County, why his parents could not have a car like the other families.

When he left home at age 18 to work at a lumber mill, Miller took this wonderment with him. It got him into trouble with his family.

Miller used his income from the job to buy a battered old car, something that was unforgivable among his strict Old Amish sect, which shuns modern conveniences.

Miller's father, a deacon in the church, barred his son's return to the family home unless he promised to get rid of the car.

"In essence, I was kicked out," he said.

Miller had only the $125 car and the clothes on his back, so he agreed to his father's demands. But when his parents let him in, he took back his word and, carrying an armload of clothes, left home for good.

As a result, he has for all practical purposes been banished by his family.

Miller turned his back, he said, on a life that would have meant [...] Amish girl, moving in [...] to his own, and [...] thing [...]

Miller went to work at a local cheese factory, where he took in milk, primarily from Amish farms.

He had thoughts about going to school once more, but felt that his slight education ruled out college. Still, when he began working as an orderly for Union Hospital in Dover, he investigated the branch campus of Kent State University at nearby New Philadelphia.

Miller took a test to make up for his lack of a high school diploma and enrolled at the Kent State branch. As a freshman, he was introduced to such things as negative numbers for the first time.

To pay for the education, he received $1,808 in student loans and earned the rest working as a hospital orderly and for [...] care company at the same time. [...] respiratory care techni[...] tions caused his [...] quarter [...]

Beacon
The Sunday Magazine of the Akron Beacon Journal, June 25, 1978

Fresh from a one-room Amish schoolhouse, Bert Miller made it through Kent State—and now he's shooting to become a doctor. His folks are plenty mad.

May 22, 1979

Dear Mr. Miller,

Our family was interested in The Cincinnati Enquirer (May 20, 1979) article concerning your endeavors to attain a medical degree. Congratulations! on being accepted by the University of Cincinnati Medical School.

My husband was in General Practice in Orrville, Ohio 1968-1972. and at present is in a group pediatric practice in Cincinnati: He is a 1965 graduate of U.C. Medical School. We are both Mennonite background and Don, also, worked hard and long years to get his medical education

Finally to the point on this letter - We would like to assist you in finding living quarters, having some home-cooked meals occasionally and letting you be part of our "family." We belong to a small Mennonite church group which could provide you with affirmation of your goals when you get discouraged.

If you need to come to Cincinnati this summer, we usually have an extra bed available.

Give us a call so we'll be at home.

We're looking forward to hearing from you and learning to know you.

May God continue to bless you.

Sincerely,
Ann Nofziger

We have 2 children - Liane - age 9
Adam - age 8

Our home and the Mennonite Church are 10 min from U.C.

Being accepted into medical school made me even more proud of my accomplishments at Kent State. I celebrated my college graduation with my friends and classmates with no family members present. My plans to move were only vaguely underway at that point. I had a steady girlfriend, but despite being together for a while, we both knew we wouldn't continue the relationship once I moved. I had to focus on the challenges of medical school.

I sold the trailer I had lived in near Kent State's main campus and got rid of almost everything I owned, which wasn't all that much. I only took what fit into my car: clothes, a TV, a toaster, a twin mattress, and some basic necessities. The only Amish possessions I still couldn't bear to part with were my hat and suit. They had long since stopped fitting me; I had filled out from the wiry eighteen-year-old I was when I left the community.

I packed a few suitcases and boxes into my Pontiac Grand Prix and squeezed my twin mattress in over the top of the seats. Of course, the mattress stuck out the window. I must have looked like some hillbilly on a lark, but I didn't care. I was heading out for an adventure. As I pulled away from Kent with the mattress hanging out, I remember thinking I hope it doesn't rain. Seeing such an overstuffed car on the road today, I would laugh at it, but at the time it seemed the perfectly natural thing to do.

I headed to Cincinnati thinking I would find an apartment in a day—oh, the naïveté of youth.

Berlin only had a few thousand people; after my datt

threw me out of his house, I had easily found a place to live. During my first two years at the Kent State branch campus in New Philadelphia, I rented a room from an elderly widow. Once at the main campus, I bought a house trailer, renting one of the bedrooms to help offset expenses. The number-one priority was always maximizing my limited income.

By contrast, Cincinnati was huge! This was my first big-city experience. I realized that I didn't even know how to find an appropriate neighborhood, much less choose an apartment. The local newspaper listed hundreds of ads for apartments and the rent was far higher than I was used to. I spent the first night with the parents of my friend Mike Sleutz, about an hour outside the city, where I pulled my mattress out of the car and slept in the living room. That night I realized I needed a better plan.

Initially, I hadn't thought a lot about the many messages of support I had received in response to the newspaper article. But the apartment hunt looked too big to handle alone. I reached out for help.

The first people I called were the Nofzigers. They were excited to get my call and took me in as if I were a long-lost relative. They directed me to the suburb of Clifton as a safe, affordable area near the school. They also showed me around the city. It was the start of a long-term friendship.

———

That newspaper article didn't just have an impact on my move to Cincinnati; it's followed me throughout my life. Now I live in Dothan, Alabama, where my wife, Pat, volunteers at our church. I never could have guessed that the story followed me even there some forty years later.

Pat was making a quilt for our soon-to-be-born grandson and asked for some help from one of her church contacts.

"I've pieced together a quilt for my baby grandson, but I have no idea how to quilt it. Do you know anyone who could help me?" she asked one of the church staff.

"Oh sure. Faye Skaburn will know how to do that. Let me give you her phone number."

My wife arranged to meet with Faye before church the next Sunday. Even though Faye was going on 90, she was still sharp as a tack and regularly drove from her home in the country to attend church services. She was more than happy to share her knowledge of quilt making.

During the course of the conversation, Faye and my wife talked about how they each ended up living in Dothan and attending our church. Pat said, "My husband is an emergency room physician, and when we moved down here from Ohio, he started working in the ER at Flowers Hospital and Dale Medical Center. He often doesn't come to Sunday services because he is on duty at the hospital. His shifts are usually twelve hours."

"Which part of Ohio did you come from?" Faye asked. "I used to live up there."

"We lived in Wooster before moving here. It's near Holmes County, where the Amish do some amazing quilting. Even though my husband grew up Amish, I never learned how to do it. Six kids kept us pretty busy!"

"Wow, what a coincidence! I remember years ago reading an article about an Amish boy who went to medical school. It was in one of the Ohio newspapers." Faye had quite a memory!

"Really? That's most likely my husband. There was an article written about him that was in the paper. He never says how proud he is of his accomplishments, but I can't imagine coming from where he came from to be where he is now."

Smiling with excitement, Faye said, "Oh my! Is he the Albert Miller who was in the *Beacon Journal* and went to Kent State? I talked about that article a lot with my sister. She thinks he's a rock star. We thought his story was fascinating!"

"Yep, he must be. I can't imagine there are too many articles about Amish youth heading off to medical school," my wife said with a smile.

As if she were discussing a celebrity, Faye asked, "My goodness! Do you think I could meet your husband sometime?"

"Why, of course!" Pat said with a good-natured laugh, thinking how sweet it was that Faye had such interest in her husband. She came home very excited to tell me her quilting story.

"Who would think that forty-plus years later that article would be so clear in someone's memory, someone I never even met? That is just awesome!" I said.

The next Sunday I was not scheduled in the ER and had the great pleasure of meeting Faye, who was indeed very impressed to meet me. The experience reminded me, with pride, in how far I had come. The twists and turns of life never cease to amaze me.

A DAUGHTER'S JOURNEY

As we move throughout life our family shifts. People often focus on the more traditional means of adding family like when people get married or have a child, but family doesn't have to be related by blood alone. Family is who we choose to make a part of our community. I often think it is unfortunate that American society encourages so much individualism. I prefer to see community as the people we gather around us to make our lives richer, and I think this is done with a whole host of diverse communities.

Living far from family, I have learned to rely on the family I choose and to make sure I am dependable to them too. My family has always been ever-widening. I know the pain and loneliness that come from holidays and special occasions spent alone, not by choice, so people are always welcome where I am. This has led me to meet amazing people. In turn, a number of people as well have opened their homes to me when I am new somewhere.

Sometimes the family who gets us best are the people we choose and who in turn choose to constantly show up, not by blood obligation, but by choice. I think the world would be much better if we all sought out and found our community so we could thrive and help others do the same. For, in the end, we are much stronger as a team than we are as individuals.

CAMELOT AND DR. SEUSS

I hadn't applied to the school as a minority student, but that was how the University of Cincinnati ultimately accepted me. The idea of being a minority shocked me.

Merriam-Webster defines *minority* as "3a: a part of a population differing from others in some characteristics and often subjected to differential treatment; b: a member of a minority group."

By that definition, I guess I can be classified as a minority. I can see how the Amish's distinct dress and lifestyle, including education only through eighth grade, count as different, plus the community life is so unlike mainstream society. I hadn't ever considered myself disadvantaged; I had just always overcome the obstacles before me. However, the university considered anyone who had not had the same opportunities as others to be a minority. And it was true, I hadn't had the educational opportunities others had. I didn't want to look a gift horse in the mouth, so I accepted minority status without question. It meant I could go to medical school, and that was my dream.

Minority students had to arrive on campus six weeks before

the start of medical school classes to attend prep courses that covered what the school expected of them. These courses outlined the overall basics of classes and study skills, stressing the importance of working in teams. These initial classes helped us learn how to navigate what was to come.

A number of the students wondered why a normal-looking white person like me was in their group. Part of our process, in the beginning, was sharing our background and why and how we got to medical school. At first, I felt a bit uncomfortable and awkward, but once they heard my story the group readily accepted me.

The differences between my cultural upbringing and mainstream society were often glaring. Part of our medical school initiation and welcome included an inaugural speech delivered by one of the administrative faculty members. He made frequent references to Camelot and welcomed us as knights to the medicinal round table. I had no idea what or who Camelot was.

"Who is this Camelot the speaker keeps mentioning?" I whispered to a classmate near me.

"How do you not know what Camelot is?" was the response.

It quickly became apparent that if I wanted to fit in, I was going to have to be more selective about who I asked about pop culture. I slowly gained trust in a few people who could explain the missing links and finer points of classic American culture.

Finding a place to fit in was something I created on my own. I wanted people to judge me for myself, by my abilities, so I rarely told people about my background right away. Instead, I waited until I felt accepted and comfortable enough that my story would not change my friends' and colleagues' views of me as a person.

To save money on insurance and maintenance I sold my car and, for the first two years of medical school, walked everywhere I needed to go. I found a studio apartment in a neighborhood that was reasonably safe but definitely wasn't elite living. I constantly heard sirens at night but soon got used to the disruption. A part-time job as a respiratory therapist at Holmes Hospital just covered my living expenses.

Classes were hard, but not harder than I had expected. The amount of time dedicated to school, though, was much greater than during my undergraduate studies. As an undergraduate, I managed to hold a full-time job, study, and still pass with good grades. That was not possible in medical school, which required six to eight hours of class per day. Then I still had to study, complete projects, and write papers.

For lectures, classmates worked in teams. Because not everyone grasps concepts the same way, one person took notes on lectures for a specific class, transcribed them, and passed them to the rest of the team. Another person was responsible for notes in a different class. Even if we weren't in charge of transcribing a lecture, the whole team showed up for class. Some students did skip classes, but I don't think I could have made it through medical school without attending the lectures. The notes each student took provided a summary and highlights of the lecture, allowing all of us in the group to benefit.

At the start of medical school, we were introduced to our anatomy lab partners and our cadaver. Two other minority students were in my anatomy group. My partner and I named our cadaver Franklin. Naming their cadaver was something students did to make dissecting a dead body tolerable. Each group of four students shared one of six cadavers for the duration of the course.

While each group dissected and learned about their own cadaver, we all compared the different cadavers. Some of them had great anatomy, others not so much. It was important for us as doctors-in-training to learn that while all bodies are generally the same, they also differ from individual to individual. Some groups dissected better than others, and at times I thought the professor had us look at the other cadavers just to admire our classmates' skills.

Biochemistry was by far the hardest subject for me. It focused on the details of how the body handles substances and how drugs work—or not—in different cases. It was clearly important, so I relied a lot on my study group to learn effectively.

Classes were long and lasted all day, and study groups were essential. The school encouraged us to pick our own groups because we would spend a lot of time together. The four people in my group all ended up being good buddies. In addition to studying, when we had a little spare time we sometimes went out to eat or to the movies. Since we were pretty poor, many of our hangout sessions involved getting together at each other's apartment to make chili or hotdogs. A number of reasonably priced restaurants were also near the medical school.

Our two favorite cheap college restaurants in the area were Emanon (No Name spelled backward) and Clifton Cafe. I still ate at home when possible—mac and cheese, chow mein noodles, hot dogs, peanut butter and jelly sandwiches, ham and cheese sandwiches, Cheerios, and eggs with bacon on toast made economical meals.

Another group of friends evolved from my part-time job. One evening one of them hosted a party, at which they started talking about Dr. Seuss and Green Eggs and Ham. I wondered who this famous doctor was.

"Who is this Dr. Seuss? What made him so famous?" I asked.

I got a lot of confused looks and laughs.

"You mean you have never had green eggs and ham?" a friend asked.

"I didn't know eggs could be green," I said.

"Aw, sweety, he's a children's author," said my current girlfriend, saving me from further embarrassment. Later she invited me to her house for breakfast and dyed eggs and ham green for me as she read me the story.

Who would have thought Dr. Seuss was not a real doctor at all? Once I realized I could find his other books at the local library, I went and read them to understand what all the hoopla was about. I was still confused about how he got the title of doctor or why he was so famous, but years later found his books magical to read to my own children.

A DAUGHTER'S DISTINCTIONS

The concept of a minority is unique around the world and in different places. Often I am a minority as a foreigner, American, or even as a white person in some countries, where I have lived. Through all of it, like my dad, I hope for people to judge me as a person and on my abilities, not on my background.

In some senses, I share many of the same attributes as first-generation immigrants, since my dad never got the 'classic American dad' culture that white America propagates in the films. Growing up, I struggled to get my dad to understand the importance of not just paying for my swim team suit but showing up to the competitions. For him fathers provide, and it took years to work on the emotional connection we have now that I was more interested in building.

Growing up I never felt like I fit in. I saw things differently, my relatives were different. Different languages were ok for me, not scary. I didn't understand the lives of many of my peers that 'looked' like me, but then again maybe that is just part of being a teenager, feeling out of place.

The fact that half my family was Amish was not something to brag about as a kid where I am from, as people tended to look at them as backward and consider them ignorant. I knew this wasn't true, but I didn't have the words in my youth to counter other people's ideas yet. It took me years to grow into an adult that understood the pride that comes with the Amish values that actually were instilled in me in different ways.

The value of community was something my father fostered in me and that I grew up loving. Our door was a revolving portal for friends, and friends of friends. No one ever knocked when I was growing up and we always had food for fifteen even though there were only eight of us who officially lived there. I loved the fact that family back then was whoever was home, and it is something I have integrated into my life today. Here in Brazil, my family is full of Brazilians, Syrians, Americans, Indians, Colombians, Chileans, Venezuelans, Italians, and people from many other countries.

Personally, I do consider my dad a minority at the time he applied to Medical School. He had an 8th-grade education and had been kept in a bubble most of his life. His culture, religion, and ethnicity were unique to less than half a million people at the time. Regardless of where you come from, it is not an easy thing to do what no one else is doing, especially when you come from a community that doesn't value it.

While I do consider that my dad was a minority growing up I do not consider myself to be one, so it shocked me that some people considered that. Since I wasn't raised Amish, I always considered myself 'regular American' whatever that means. (The melting of many cultures smashed together.) Once at a job interview, I am not sure how my Amish relatives came up but they did. The interviewer turned to me at the end of the interview and said, "You should really mark yourself on the applications as a minority, your life is fascinating, and then you would count as a minority and female hire for some companies." It was one of my first real salary-paying job interviews, and I was stunned into silence.

But it made me think. Is a minority based on wealth? Color? Ethnic heritage? On your lifestyle? Or on one's point of view? If so, whose? If it is based on normalcy, what is that metric? Or is it based on one's own personal experiences? Can you be less of a minority or less ethnic if you are affected less by stereotypes or racism?

I would consider myself more of a minority as a woman than ever as a descendent of the Amish. I have been denied more opportunities for being female than ever for having Amish heritage. Not allowed on the boys' sports teams, or in Boy Scouts (Who wants to learn to bake cookies if the boys get to go camping?), and denied roles where the response was "we are just not sure if the team would follow a female leader well."

Despite the interviewer's advice, I've never marketed myself as a minority, because I always felt I had all the privileges I needed to succeed.

It was good to have study groups that became friends, especially as without them my holidays would have been lonely. One of my classmates always made sure I had a place to go for the holidays. Over Thanksgiving, our group sometimes made a turkey dinner, or I went to Mike Sluetz's house. I learned that family doesn't just mean blood relations. Sometimes it is the family you choose that shows up when you need them most.

In our second year, we started to do physical exams on each other in class. Then we had to learn how to interview patients effectively, starting with each other. By the end of our first two years, the school had taught us all the basic science, how to talk to patients, and make analogies. As I studied the diseases, I sometimes thought I had a disease just from reading the symptoms, even though I wasn't even sick.

> Common symptoms include but are not limited to shaking and chills, high fever, profuse sweating, headaches, nausea, vomiting, abdominal pain, diarrhea, anemia, muscle pain, convulsions, coma, and/or bloody stool. Some infected patients may not show all these symptoms, or some symptoms may remain dormant.

Every student doctor tends to go through at least a minor hypochondriac stage, wondering *Do I have this? Or wait. Maybe it's malaria?* Headaches, check. Muscle pain, check. Profuse sweating, check. Trouble sleeping, check. *I could have malaria!* The panic sent me racing for a thermometer. Maybe I got it from a patient last night. The sweat seemed to cool me down. *Do I have the chills now? Dear Lord, I might die!*

"Albert, what are you doing?" one study buddy asked.

"I think I have malaria. I have some of the symptoms: muscle pain, and . . ."

She said, "Have you been to a tropical region lately? Malaria is a tropical disease and you get it from a mosquito bite."

"Oh, I guess not then," I said, retreating into my book to read about other diseases I could stress over.

Prior to the internet and WebMD, patients typically just panicked about their symptoms until they talked to a doctor, who made the diagnosis based on extensive training, patients' symptoms, and an examination. Now a whole world of information—much of it, at best uninformed, and at worst, incorrect—is available with just a few clicks. Patients often show up in a doctor's office already convinced they know what they are suffering from. Usually, they are wrong.

LEARNING TO FLY

Years earlier, I had promised myself I would learn to fly but had never had either the time or the money for it. One day in medical school a radical idea dawned on me: As a doctor later in life, I would likely have a lot more money but less time. I needed to optimize my free time now. I went to investigate how much flying lessons cost, did a few calculations, and determined that if I saved here and there, I could fly once or twice a month. That seemed totally doable; I decided to treat myself!

My flight instructor was Pat Kissel. The two of us flew in a small two-seater plane, which practically felt like I was flying myself. The wind rushed by and the propeller noise roared in my ears despite the headphones we wore to communicate.

Flying involves a lot of studying—not just to chart courses but to understand the physics of flight, how to use the instruments, and adjust them effectively for flight conditions. When I flew with the instructor, both of us had access to the controls of the plane to prevent any issues.

One of the first things Kissel taught me was how to recover if the plane stalls.

He explained, "We use these small planes because it's easier to learn how to recover and straighten them out if the plane stalls. It won't stall out of nowhere; you'll have some warning, but you need to think on your feet. Before the plane stalls, a loud stall horn sounds, and then the plane will quiver and shake. Try it."

I tried to stall the plane by adjusting the rudder and pulling the nose of the plane up, but I was too nervous to let it go into a full stall.

After several tries, Kissel took back control of the plane. "Dammit, Bert, I said stall this thing! Don't be afraid to stall the plane. You have to know what it feels like so you learn how to recover." The stall horn sounded, and he held the plane through the quivering that followed until the plane started to drop. Then he deftly restarted the engine and recovered back to normal flight.

Then he said, "OK, Bert, now you do it." I was still a little anxious, but this time I did it.

Initially, I thought I would fly once a week. I quickly realized that was no way to learn; each time I took off it seemed as though I had to relearn everything from the week before. My strategy needed to change. I saved enough money to fly ten straight hours and learned to trust myself in the airplane. After I gained that confidence, I waited until I saved some more money. Eventually, I was flying almost twice a week.

"Don't be scared of the plane. Make the plane do what you want it to do, or it will kill you," Kissel reminded me. "I won't let you get your pilot's license until I think you're comfortable with the basic equipment and maneuvers of the airplane. I have to know that when you're in the clouds and you have to fly blind with just the instruments, you know what to do."

We practiced takeoffs and landings first, then landing without power. Next, we worked with blinders, flying only on instruments, to mimic being in the clouds before flying through the clouds for real. I found that the most exhilarating part of flight training.

"What's the first thing you do when you're flying visually along at 1,500 feet and the ground is less than 1,000 feet below you, and you hit a cloud?" he asked.

"I'm not sure. What should I do?"

"Instinctively you want to go down, but you have to go up to be safe because you don't know what's below the cloud. Then you call flight control for help and file an IFR flight plan to be safe. And then you get back out of the clouds and land. Now let's practice." Later on I would be very glad for this instrument flight training with the initial pilot license.

On one flight to Texas, I was on a VFR-filed flight plan with a scheduled refueling stop in Little Rock, Arkansas. VFR flying meant I was responsible for keeping myself away from other airplanes and clouds, so clear visibility was essential, but somehow I got into some clouds. I thought I saw a break ahead of me, but actually, it was a trick of the light. What I thought was the blue sky was in fact a reflection of light from a lower cloud. My clear blue skies turned to opaque white walls.

In my head, I heard Kissel encouraging me. "Fly straight and climb."

I flew straight and climbed up until I was above the clouds and felt in control again. Then I radioed the nearest flight control center to request assistance. I clicked the microphone to the last control center I had communicated with.

"88 Victor, Traffic Control Center," I said, indicating I had a request and waiting for their response.

The response came almost immediately. "88 Victor, go ahead."

"88 Victor accidentally entered clouds and I need assistance. Requesting vectors to the nearest airport I can land at. I am currently above a thin cloud layer, but approximately thirty minutes ago was below the cloud layer and passed over an airport."

"88 Victor, we have you in radar contact." The control tower saw me and was able to give directions. "The clouds are reported as dense ahead of you. Would you like to return to Papa Papa Gulf? That appears to be the airport you saw thirty minutes ago."

"Requesting vectors to Papa Papa Gulf. Providing the clouds are thin enough, I plan to land there."

"88 Victor, turn heading 190 vectors to Papa Papa Gulf." I continued flying for fifteen minutes until another message came through.

"88 Victor, turn heading 210. Your airport is ten miles at twelve o'clock. Report insight."

In another five miles, I reported, "Airport is insight. Clouds are scattered and I am able to make a VFR landing."

"As you descend below 2,500 feet, we will lose radar contact. Cleared for the approach. This is an uncontrolled airport. Radio Frequency 118.7. If unable to land, call back for further assistance."

That time I landed safely and waited out the weather. As a pilot, I quickly learned that things don't always turn out the way I expected, and a sudden change in weather may require quick thinking and adjusted plans. Similarly, in my job as an ER physician, I find sudden changes in a patient's condition require quick thinking, re-evaluating, and changing a treatment plan.

MARY JANE

I met Mary Jane, whom I quickly started to call MJ, at the Nofziger's house during my first year at the University of Cincinnati. She liked me a lot from the start. When I learned to fly, I took her up in the airplane. Flying with someone was always much more fun than flying alone.

Despite being in the English world, I still didn't understand the finer points of functioning in it. Sometimes it seemed that I would forever struggle to fit into mainstream America. MJ taught me so many things about American culture—from what to wear and how to combine colors, to cultural references I didn't understand. She helped me understand and develop common social skills.

"Don't lean on the table when eating, Bert."

"If you need to excuse yourself from the table, put the cloth napkin on the chair or folded next to your plate."

"When you set a place table for dinner, the napkin goes on the left side."

She was an RN and studying to be a nurse anesthetist. Classes and our busy schedules meant we were nothing more than good friends for most of those first years. Then she moved to Pittsburgh to study for a year, and we saw each other even less frequently, though we stayed in touch, talking on the phone, and sometimes she came to visit me.

With my pilot and medical studies occupying most of my time, I didn't think too much about the future. I was too busy trying to accomplish my immediate goals. Then on one of her visits, MJ unexpectedly suggested that we get married. She could be eccentric at times, but she was a strong support system for me. I felt we could help each other. We toyed with the idea of marriage but didn't talk about it seriously at first. The thought of marriage lingered in the backdrop of our friendship for several years.

PRACTICING MEDICINE

While the first two years of medical school were based on classroom learning, with basic lectures on physiology, anatomy, and other topics, the next two years actually allowed us to walk in the shoes of doctors. The only significant clinical part in the first years was learning how to work up a complete history, do physical exams, and interview patients. Armed with this knowledge, we started to learn how to develop a differential diagnosis and treatment plan for each patient's specific illnesses. The second two years showed us the clinical side of medicine, although these still involved a lot of book learning and research. During that time we rotated through the various medical specialties and learned how to use the book knowledge gained in our first two years. Our teachers were no longer mere classroom professors, but actual physicians.

During these rotations, we were assigned patients and were

expected to do a complete history and physical, develop a differential diagnosis and create a workup plan of what lab work, x-rays, and tests to order. We presented the plan to the resident physician and attending physician for their comments and criticisms, then ordered the agreed-upon lab tests and x-rays. Our notes were written in the patient's chart, but not made official until a resident or attending physician signed off on the entry.

I learned to research any disease topic that I was not completely familiar with before arriving at a plan to present to the residents and attending physicians. In this learning phase, the teaching staff, residents, and attending physicians frequently challenged students' thought processes and asked a lot of questions to help students be more confident in their decisions. These two years were when we learned to truly practice medicine. By this time most of us had already decided on a specialty that we wanted to pursue. Regardless, most of us, myself included, found that we actually liked nearly all of the specialties and many of us changed our plans based on our experience in areas we hadn't previously considered.

When we started clinic rotation, beginning my third year, I had to quit my job. I simply didn't have time to manage both rotation and a job. Unfortunately, we didn't get paid for clinic time since we were still students. Only residents who had graduated from medical school could work billable hours. During clinic time, students literally had to pay to be on staff. To cover expenses, I had to borrow even more money in my last two years. I had gotten some grant money from the University of Cincinnati, supplemented with a variety of government-sponsored student loans. Those loans took me fifteen years to pay off.

As a clinical student, I always tried to have all my rounds done before meeting with the resident and attending physician to avoid embarrassment. I prepared a complete list of differential diagnoses and the diseases that I could rule out based on specific test results. I also had a list of any additional tests needed to confirm or deny possible diagnoses, if necessary. I preferred to be over-prepared.

It's not always easy to diagnose a problem the first time around. Misdiagnosis is not uncommon even today, and that is why it is important for doctors to have a differential diagnosis, which offers several options to test. I was always good at deductive reasoning and enjoyed trying to analyze and figure out the problem. When I first started clinical rotations, I carried books with me for quick references, such as the *Infectious Disease Guide* and the *Washington Manual*, to help me develop a thorough differential diagnosis and arrive at a treatment plan.

Today, doctors don't use books much. The process has become far simpler. We hop on UptoDate.com or Hippocrate.org, online resources that instantly offer detailed information about diseases and help doctors to arrive at a differential diagnosis faster. These resources are constantly kept current and are much easier to use than bulky reference books. They also allow doctors to chat with other doctors via message boards for some of the rarer diagnoses. It is amazing how technology has changed medicine since I was a student.

There were also many tricks of the trade to learn from other residents and doctors during clinical rotations.

"Look for the Scotty dog on the back x-rays. The bones make a picture of a dog if you are creative enough to find it. It shows that the bones are lined up normally in the lumbar spine," one resident pointed out, showing us a healthy spine x-ray.

Such analogies are common in medical practice. They help doctors quickly and easily remember crucial aspects of medicine.

On another round, I was looking over the shoulder of a resident who was examining an intestinal x-ray.

"Oh no! It looks like this guy has a big *IF*."

The other students whispered among themselves until one student finally spoke up. "What's a big IF?"

"Wow, you guys don't know?" the doctor said playfully, looking from face to confused face. "This is something we see quite often in x-rays. It's important for you to recognize it." He traced a black spot representing air or gas on the image. All the students looked horrified, thinking they had forgotten a key medical diagnostic step.

"This is what we traditionally call an *IF* or an *Impending Fart*." Childlike giggles relieved the tension in the room.

Smiling, he said, "Now, now, future doctors, a gas bubble in the rectum is no laughing matter."

Such events brought an element of fun to the intense learning and helped offset the more serious and sad things we encountered, like finding cancer and having to share that difficult news with a patient.

————

In my third year, I bought a Chevy Chevette, which I needed to get to the various hospitals and clinics for my rotations, and moved in with John Graves, a friend I met via church. We shared a two-bedroom apartment in Western Hill, farther from the school than I had lived before. It was nice to be away from the wailing of the sirens. Here the housing was more economical, but the drive was long. A car was a necessity; it was impossible for me to walk to all the different facilities where I did clinical work.

On average, I was on call and spent the night at the hospital every third night. It might seem like the workload was lighter, but it wasn't. It was exhausting. As a student, I worked directly with a resident. It was my responsibility to write up patients' histories, do their physicals, and present cases to the resident or attending doctor the next morning. The residents and attendings expected a full report on the patients and for their labs to be ready and updated by 7 or 7:30 AM at the latest, so I typically had to be on-site by at least 6 AM to finish on time. The process was grueling; however, it taught us to be thorough and develop a clear and thoughtful differential diagnosis.

As a medical student, I learned that patients come from all walks of life and cultures, and it is critical not to be judgmental. Considering my own different cultural background, and knowing the pain of being judged for personal choices, I hope I have learned to be more empathetic with patients than some of my peers. That did not, however, prevent me from being surprised and on occasion, even shocked at some of the stories I heard during patient encounters.

During my time as a clinical student, the HIV/AIDS crisis exploded. One day while working in the infectious disease specialty area, consulting on a patient, I learned he had been diagnosed with HIV.

"Sir, do you have a steady partner?"

"I just can't believe it happened to me, Doctor. I'm so careful. I mean, maybe reflecting back I can understand. But I'm so careful."

"Sir, I need to ask you, how many sexual partners have you had in the last six months?"

"Doctor, my partner and I live together. We are so careful."

"I understand that a diagnosis like this is hard to accept, but we will help you the best we can. To do that, I do need you to answer my questions as best as you can. How many sexual partners have you had in the last six months?"

"It is just my partner and me. And we are so careful. We do go to the spas once a month, sometimes more, and spend a weekend."

"How would these spas affect your diagnosis?"

"Oh, you don't know spas? That's where a bunch of gay people get together on the weekend. I guess we usually do have different partners then."

"Can you give me an estimate of how many different partners?"

"Gee, I don't know. On a weekend, there might be ten or fifteen different partners."

I asked, "Are these the same ten to fifteen people each time?"

"No, they're usually different. Sometimes I don't even know them."

After doing some quick math in my head, I said dryly, "It seems you may have had greater exposure than you thought."

I had to practically hide behind the chart so he couldn't see the look of shock on my face as I wrote down "Possibly 50–100 partners in the past year." I was used to numbers below ten in Ohio during that era, and such large numbers took me by surprise.

One of the secret arts of being a good doctor is never looking surprised, no matter what patients say. Being judgmental will only hinder the doctor-patient relationship. But some weird things show up! A professional must act as though a jam jar, a Scotch glass, a bottle, a softball, or a vibrator lodged in a patient's rectum are all perfectly normal. I have seen all these and more. The story each patient tells me about how these objects got there never gets a response, no matter how shocked I may be.

A DAUGHTER'S IMPRESSION

Never being shocked is a true skill. I have learned as well to listen rather than judge right away as a teacher. Some of my teenage students were constantly trying to shock me with information that might have shocked their parents. Mostly about who they were dating, or some of their misadventures. Rather than be quick to judge, it was important to first listen and then attempt to guide them towards a safer path when necessary or to remind them to use caution as they went about experimenting. At times when required, I would call in professional back up if it was essential for the student's mental or physical health.

My dad's non-judgemental approach to being a doctor is something I admire. One of the hardest parts for me leaving home was realizing that not all doctors feel this way.

Especially as a woman I have had some awful experiences with doctors who do not focus on treating and helping to heal patients. Rather I have run into misogynistic doctors who would rather hold their 'superior knowledge' over your head, shame women for having sex, or misdiagnose women because they won't listen to a woman's symptoms long enough to understand.

Listening is at the heart of all the greatest advances forward in my opinion, whether it is in a relationship, as a teacher, or as a doctor. As I have traveled it has been hard to find a doctor who always listens. That is why I still use my dad half the time via the cellphone as my primary doctor, for me, my loved ones, and friends. No matter what transpires, he's not shocked and he tries to help.

A good doctor has to know how to talk to people and deliver sad news in a concerning and compassionate manner. One of the most difficult things to learn is how to tell someone a loved one has died. It's almost impossible to be a doctor and not have to do this at least once, and for some doctors, it is a regular occurrence. Sometimes the family sees the patient's heart stop. These families know what has happened, even if they don't want to accept the truth. Other times, the family has no idea that death is imminent. These are the hardest cases. The person was alive when they left home, and now they are behind a closed door.

What happened in between? Doctors need to find out.

1. Get the background story: "Can you tell me when you last saw your husband?"

"What? Is he OK? I saw him this morning when he left for work, just like every morning. He was fine! What happened?"

"Did you speak to him throughout the day at all?"

"No, but that's normal. What's going on?"

2. Let them know what happened: "Well, ma'am, unfortunately, your husband didn't make it to work today. He was hit by a car on Route 83 near the lumber mill. We don't know exactly how long he was there, but someone called it in around 9 AM. He was rushed here but had already lost a lot of blood. Whoever hit him didn't stop to call for help."

"Is he OK? Is he going to be OK?"

3. Tell them what procedures were done: "Ma'am, his heart stopped three times. Once in the ambulance, and twice here at the hospital. We were able to get his heartbeat back the first two times, but the third time we couldn't restart it despite CPR, a blood transfusion, and medication. His injuries were too severe and he'd lost too much blood. We were unable to revive him, and he has passed on. I am so sorry I have to tell you this."

4. Offer any comfort you can: Sometimes family members grab at the doctor or nurse, collapsing into hysterical tears. Other times they need a hug, or maybe they just slump into a chair in shock. Some people get angry and shout and scream. Whatever their reaction, the words don't ever get any easier.

Nothing either a doctor or the nursing staff can offer will ever make up even a tiny percentage of what was lost, however, we try to provide as much comfort as possible.

———

During the first year of clinical rotations, students may be allowed to scrub in on a surgery and may even help with simple tasks like suturing the skin, the final step in closing the surgical wound. A surgeon once told me as I was closing for him, "Remember, your suture is the only part the patient sees, so do it well, because it will reflect on me!"

By my fourth year, I had mastered the skills needed to

provide a thorough history, physical exam, develop a differential diagnosis, and provide a treatment plan for the resident and attending physicians. Occasionally, if a supervising physician liked and trusted me, I was allowed to perform part of the surgery under their direct supervision.

Once I did an appendectomy, removed an appendix, working under the direct supervision of the physician. The patient was required to give consent for me to do the procedure.

The attending surgeon, Dr. Silverman, looked at me and said, "Do you want to do this one?"

"Sure," I said, both excited and a little nervous.

"You've helped with enough of these that you know how to do it," he said with an encouraging smile.

I asked the nurse, "Please hand me a number twelve blade."

Before making the cut, I marked where I would make the incision in the air above the patient, which Dr. Silverman confirmed as the correct placement.

I made the incision in the skin and gave the blade back to the nurse. "Please hand me curved scissors."

These scissors are used to dissect the soft tissue in the abdominal wall. I worked my way through the small layer of fatty tissue to the abdominal wall muscles and glanced at Dr. Silverman. "I will now separate the fibers of the muscle without cutting them, using the blunt end of the scissors."

"Go ahead," he confirmed.

I worked my way through the muscle fibers to the abdominal lining.

"I will incise the peritoneum with the scissors."

"OK," the doctor said.

I requested a hemostat from the nurse, which I used to retract the peritoneum to make sure it was free of any portion of the small bowel, then used the scissors to open the peritoneum.

At this point I inserted my gloved fingers into the incision and set retractors on each side to pull the abdominal wall apart, exposing the large and small bowels as well as the appendix. As I finished with each instrument, I returned it to the nurse, who discarded it on a table.

Inside I saw the red, angry-looking appendix. The inflammation of the appendix confirmed our diagnosis of appendicitis, which was later confirmed by the pathologist.

"Two hemostats, please." These instruments are placed right next to each other with just enough room to allow for separation of the appendix using an electrocautery device, a thin blade that cuts by heating. The heat both prevents bleeding and sterilizes the ends of the incision, helping to prevent infection. The appendix is placed into a container to be sent to pathology. A ligature suture is then placed at the base where the appendix was removed, and the hemostat is removed.

Dr. Silverman and I examined the operative site. He looked at me with a smile. "Good job, Doctor. You are ready to close."

Closing is the easiest part, the part that I had been allowed to do many times over the past year. Each layer is closed separately, starting with the peritoneum. The muscles are not sutured but are allowed to heal naturally. Lastly, the subcutaneous tissues and skin are closed.

GRADUATION DAY

I graduated on a bright and sunny Saturday, July 11, 1983. I'd been looking forward to that day for the past four years. Even longer than that, when I thought about it.

Yet as I scanned the crowd of happy faces ready to celebrate with my classmates, a cloud temporarily eclipsed my pride. Not one of all those parents, grandparents, and family members was there for me. Not one member of my family—two parents, four brothers, and six sisters—came to celebrate the culmination of all my sleepless nights, studying, trials, and tribulations that finally resulted in me being one of the 192 classmates who survived the grueling doctoral process to earn a medical degree.

I brushed that cloud aside. I wouldn't dwell on that, because it was my day to celebrate my accomplishments, despite all the obstacles. And while I might not have a single member of my family there, I had friends, study partners, and professors who recognized what it took for someone who never went to high school to be awarded a medical degree. These people were part of my new and expanding family. They showed up when it counted.

I sat there, proud in my black gown and red cap with its

red tassel. I had bought a new suit for the occasion and wore it under my gown, and for once felt very comfortable. This, finally, was the moment I had waited for. I was almost a doctor. We sat alphabetically in rows, waiting to receive our diplomas. MJ, the Nofzigers, Mike and Kathy Sleutz, and a few other friends were there to support me. Even Eli and Vesta Hochstetler, my Holmes County Post High friends, had come.

Don and Ann Nofzigers were kind enough to throw a party for me after the ceremony. It was a small, intimate affair at their house, with a lot of mutual friends. I felt so proud to have that recognition from those who had supported me on my journey to accomplish this dream.

PART 4
SCIENCE, FAITH AND GRACE

MARRIAGE

MJ came down from Pittsburgh for my medical school graduation, and that was when we officially decided that we wanted a life and a family together. We were already good friends. What could go wrong in our marriage? I was moving to Cleveland, Ohio, for my general surgery internship, and MJ would finish her studies at the end of August and had lined up a job there as well. A few weeks before graduation we had gone to Cleveland to find an apartment.

I announced our plan to the Nofzigers, our long-time friends.

"Bert, do you know what you're getting into?"

"Are you sure you want to do that?"

"Yes, I know she has her issues. When she can't talk to her parents, then she talks to me, and I seem to be able to help her. And she helps me. I think we complement each other."

We got married on September 30, 1983, at St. Pascal's Church in Cleveland. The service was a very small, non-traditional wedding because we knew that few people would attend. MJ wore a new dress, but we had none of the traditional bridal frills and partying. MJ's parents attended, along with her cousins Joe and Eileen Ditchman, her sister, Kathy, Kathy's husband, and her brother Joel. No one from my family came. The Nofzigers and Mike and Kathy Sleutz represented me.

Afterward, we had a simple reception dinner at a nearby

restaurant. We decided to delay our honeymoon until I could get some more time off, and instead spent the weekend at an inn in the mountains of eastern Pennsylvania.

We had a great time that weekend and came home Sunday evening, ready to go to work the next day. Later that same evening, I walked into the living room to find MJ sitting on the floor in the corner, facing the wall. She didn't look at me—only stared at the wall.

"Bert, I want to talk to you."

"Sure, MJ, what do you need?"

"There are a couple of things I need you to know."

"Like?"

"Just because I'm your wife doesn't mean I'm going to cook for you or do your laundry. You can do that on your own." She paused and I wasn't really sure what to say to that. I hadn't expected such a sudden ultimatum.

"Here are the rules: You will never call or invite my parents here without my permission. Is that clear?"

"Sure, MJ. That's fine."

I thought her behavior was a little weird, but that seemed to be the end of it. I figured she was just adjusting to our new relationship. Besides, I worked a lot of hours, and at the time it didn't seem to matter too much.

We were married for only a few weeks when she started disappearing, typically on the weekends, without telling me where she was going.

I still don't know where she went, though I guessed Pittsburgh to visit friends there. I had a sneaking suspicion she was seeing her ex-boyfriend. Sometimes I answered the phone when he called. I also heard rumors from a medical photographer that she was having an affair with one of the doctors at the hospital where she worked.

I wasn't sure what to do. I didn't like her behavior, but she was moody and quick to anger if I confronted her. I didn't know how to handle either the rumors or her disappearances. I knew people could be judgmental, so I just ignored the situation and prayed that things would work out.

One day I finally got up the courage to address the situation.

"Mary Jane, I don't mind if you want some time alone. I do think I have the right to know where you are going, though, and when you will come home." It seemed like a reasonable request.

She went into a rage and tried to slap me, screaming, "You have no right to know where I'm going and what I'm doing. If you want to control me like that I'll never come back." She slammed the door and left. I breathed a sigh of relief— the first of many to come.

I was never sure whether she even knew what she did when she left the apartment. Sometimes she had what I called spells, getting a cold, distant, glassy look in her eyes. During those spells, she was utterly unpredictable. I quickly learned it wasn't a good idea to say anything to her then. Her actions made me almost afraid of her. I prayed about her behavior and kept hoping it would resolve itself. I knew before we were married that she had some coping and mood issues, but usually, I could talk her out of them. These new spells were beyond me.

Some of her friends knew about her moods. Joe and Eileen, her cousins, called frequently to check on her. Sometimes when I answered I told them she wasn't home. That seemed simpler than trying to explain her behavior, but eventually, it backfired.

"Well, where is she?" Eileen asked.

"I don't know."

After a number of calls like this, Joe got on the phone. "What do you mean, you don't know where she is? Tell me what's going on."

"Well, Joe, to be honest, she frequently leaves and refuses to tell me where she's going or even when she'll come back. Usually, it's on a Friday and she's back on Sunday, but not always. I don't know much more than that."

"Is she OK when she comes back?" asked Joe.

"Sure, generally she just acts like nothing happened. As if she's just stepped out to the supermarket. For her, it seems pretty normal. I guess I rather assumed it was."

I don't know if they ever mentioned our conversation to MJ, but at least I wasn't the only one who knew. I honestly didn't understand how unusual it was. Since I had been raised in a completely different environment, I had relied on MJ to be my beacon for mainstream American culture. We took our late honeymoon vacation in March of the following year, the first chance I had to take time off. As we were getting ready to go to the airport, she went into one of her outbursts.

I was completely unprepared for what came next.

"Maybe we should just get a divorce," she said. After a few minutes, I managed a response.

"MJ, if that's what you want, then we can talk about it." My response shocked her. I think she thought that with my Amish background I would never consider divorce and felt that in some sense protected her. Divorce was not what I wanted and I wasn't truly considering it.

"Do you still want to go on our honeymoon?" I asked gently, breaking the silence.

"Yes, let's go," she said, almost as if a cloud had lifted.

We went to Hawaii for our honeymoon. The first night at dinner she said she had a surprise for me. I was wary, unable to imagine what it might be. Surprises could be either amazing or catastrophic with MJ, and my first thought was the conversation we'd had right before we left. *What kind of a surprise was this?*

She handed me a card. When I opened it, out fell a photograph, a blurry black-and-white image. A sonogram.

"I'm pregnant," she said.

Joy and shock rippled through me. I had always wanted to be a dad!

But then doubts crept in. *Would I really be a dad? Was the baby mine?*

Whenever MJ left for long periods, on her return she was always passionately invested in making love. *Had she done this to cover her infidelity? Did she want me to think someone else's child was mine? Was I really about to be a father?*

A DAUGHTER'S SHOCK

My dad's sudden revelation struck me like a blow to the face.

I'm writing this book with you, and you don't know if I'm actually your daughter?!

My dad said the words so nonchalantly as if mentioning that he wanted pizza for dinner. Nothing out of the ordinary here. Questions bombarded me like unsuspecting hail.

Am I his daughter, or not?

If not, whose daughter am I?

How has this never come up before?

How did he just brush over it like it's nothing? Like it's just common knowledge?

What is going on?!

I asked him to back it up a bit.

"Dad, what do you mean, you weren't sure I was your child? Whose child would I be?"

He said, "Well, to tell you the truth I was never sure if any of you were my biological children. Regardless, you are all my children. I decided that long before you were born."

Then he went on with his story as my mind reeled from this new knowledge. Suddenly I questioned everything I thought I knew about myself. I needed to talk this through with someone, but who? I didn't want to create worry with my siblings over something Dad wasn't even sure of. I had always felt like his child and didn't want to make him feel bad.

He just kept talking. But I had trouble listening that night. My mind wouldn't focus.

Hearing my father question his paternity shocked me. I had never considered the possibility that I might not be my father's daughter. To him, I always was his daughter, even before I was born, even with his doubts. His commitment to me and my siblings made me admire and love him even more than I already did. But curiosity still got the best of me.

"Dad, if you don't think I am your daughter, whose daughter do you think I am?"

"Well, I don't really know. If you want, we can do a paternity test to find out, but I always had a suspicion that your mom was still seeing her old boyfriend. All I know is that he was Jewish and his name was Mark. He lived in Pittsburgh when she lived there."

I let this information roll around in my mind for a while, musing on the implications. Wow, when I was detained at the Israeli border because they thought I was Jewish and should serve my military time, maybe it wasn't because of my big Miller nose. Maybe I really was Jewish? Could they have forced me to serve in military service there if I didn't know I was Jewish?

Would I want to meet a biological dad? If this guy had been seeing my mom then, he must have known she was pregnant, which would mean he intentionally ignored me. Or maybe he just didn't take responsibility for his actions.

Did I really need any more craziness in my life now,

at age thirty-three?

Still, these questions nagged at my brain. A friend helped me realize I never lacked a father growing up. A blood test wouldn't change my status, nor how my dad and I felt. Parenting is about who shows up, not a biological genome. That was what mattered. Deep down I'd learned this lesson years ago with my mom who had all the biological genomes and none of the will to show up and be a part of my life for the past twenty-plus years.

In the end, I asked my dad to do a DNA test just to satisfy my curiosity. We took a *23andme* test from FamilyTreeDNA.com.

If we count these as accurate. Turns out I'm his biological daughter after all. The results also indicated that my cousin on my mom's side is my half-sister. Since she has no DNA from my dad, did my aunt raise my mother's first daughter out of wedlock? Or is the site just baloney? Some things bring more questions than answers, but at some point we all stop searching further too and decide to be happy with where we are.

I needed to talk to someone about my doubts, so I went to see Father John, the priest who had married us. He and MJ were good friends since, despite her actions, she was a devout Catholic. She spent a lot of time at the church and even joined Father John at the symphony on occasion.

I scheduled an appointment to discuss my concerns with

him and get advice. The first thing I did was explain how unstable our marriage was.

"She leaves all the time. When she comes back, she always wants to have sex, but is that a cover for infidelity? I don't know. Now suddenly out of the blue, after talking about maybe getting a divorce, she tells me she's pregnant. I'm so confused. She talked about divorce and announced she was pregnant on the same day!"

"Are you going to stay married?" Father John asked.

"I think so. I wasn't raised to believe in divorce."

"Ultimately, Albert, it's like this. Any man can be a sperm donor, but not everyone can be a father. You need to decide: Does it matter to you whose sperm made the baby? Does it matter to you whether you're the biological father, or not? Then ask yourself, do you really want to know? Or do you even really want to be a father? These are all distinct questions."

Father John and I had many similar conversations until I resolved my doubts. I wanted to be a father, and I always have. I never again questioned whether the children were mine. I was their father regardless of where the sperm came from.

ONGOING CHALLENGES

I had stopped trying to force my way into family events, deciding that if my parents and siblings wanted me at weddings and other events, they would invite me. If I wasn't invited, then I didn't want to be there.

No one in my Amish family had come to my wedding. I was saddened not to have them there for the occasion, but I had learned to not set my expectations too high. The summer after our wedding, while I was doing my residency in Cleveland, I got a letter from my parents inviting me home for the annual Miller Homecoming. They said my siblings would be there but did not mention MJ. I knew invitations were tricky in my family and wanted to avoid a conflict ahead of time.

Hi Memm and Datt,

Thank you for the invitation to the Homecoming. I would love to attend. However, I noticed that my wife, MJ, is not mentioned in the invitation.

Did you remember that I got married?

I am happy to accept this invitation if she is invited as well. If she is not, then I will respectfully decline. Please let me know either way so I can plan accordingly.

Thanks,

Albert

My datt wrote back that MJ was invited as well, and that everyone would try their best to ensure that she felt welcome. He didn't fail to remind me that my visit would be difficult for them.

MJ had long known about my family issues and was curious, to say the least. I was nervous, but she went into it with the enthusiasm of a sociologist gathering data. The drive to Holmes County was awkward and uncomfortable since neither of us knew what to expect. Fortunately, my family made the effort to speak mostly in English and to make her feel comfortable. They allowed us to sit together during the event, although normally women sat on one side and men on the other. It was nice of them to extend this courtesy to us.

As always, the long tables were full of chicken, ham, mashed potatoes, and other delicious farm-grown food, with the benches lining the sides for us to sit on. The event went as well as we could have expected. MJ asked questions to help provide some conversation starters, and people took turns speaking in English so everyone could understand. After that MJ was always invited.

Early on we were only invited when the Homecoming was held at my brother John's home. My family has always maintained a relationship with my brother John; my children grew up playing with his kids. Even now, they are still the Amish cousins my children feel most comfortable with and the only set of my siblings' kids that my children all know by name.

As time went on, though, the family seemed to accept us more, and slowly my other siblings started to invite us when they hosted the reunion. Today we are invited to almost all of the Homecomings. Just a few relatives remained less open and accepting of me. The 2018 Miller Homecoming was held at my oldest sister's house, and no invitation arrived. I only found out about it in conversations with siblings after the fact.

It's comforting that this attitude has gradually changed over time, yet some things can never be recovered. Getting to know my nieces and nephews, and my children getting to know their cousins, can never truly be replaced.

On later trips, my datt sometimes intentionally caused issues by refusing to speak English, even though he was fluent in it. He insisted on speaking only Pennsylvania Dutch.

"Dad, please speak English so my wife and children can understand you."

"You should be teaching them Pennsylvania Dutch," he replied, as stubborn as ever.

"If you are speaking around my children or my wife, please do it in English. I won't talk in front of them in a language they don't understand. That's just rude."

On those days we cut the visit short. It made no sense to stay where someone intentionally made my family and me feel unwelcome.

FROM RESIDENCY TO PRACTICE

Deciding what residency I wanted was similar to applying to medical schools: a search for possible programs in my chosen specialty. I selected my top options, applied, and waited for the interview process to start. Residency applications are entered into a matching system where future residents enter a list of programs in the order of preference; the programs rank the residents in numerical order by preference. Each program has a maximum number of residents who can enter, and once that number has been reached that program is closed for the year.

At the end of medical school, students can do an internship for one year and then start in general practice. However, nearly every new doctor does a full residency training to be board-certified in a specialty.

I had initially planned to do a family practice residency, but at the end of my third year of medical school, I changed my choice to orthopedics. A one-year internship in general surgery is required before entering an orthopedics residency. The match program assigned me to the general surgery internship program at Huron Road Hospital in Cleveland.

In November 1984, during my general surgery internship, I interviewed for orthopedic residency options. I was in New York for an orthopedic residency interview when, in the middle of the interview, the receptionist came in and told me I had a phone call.

Almost no one but MJ knew where I was. When I got on the phone my wife said, "Bert, my water broke. Pam's taking me to Mount Sinai Hospital. Please meet me there."

I hung up the phone and said, "My wife is about to give birth to our first child! Thank you for your time. I appreciate the interview, but I need to leave now."

"Congratulations!" the interviewers said as I headed out the door. It was hard to keep my excitement, and my driving, under control as I sped back to Cleveland to meet my first child. As it turned out, there was no need to rush. Elizabeth took her time coming—nearly thirty-six hours of labor. She was born the next day—the most exciting day of my life.

I was ecstatic about being a father. Elizabeth was so tiny and precious, with the classic giant Miller nose. Being a father made me so proud, even more than graduating from medical school. Sleepless nights were not uncommon for me as a doctor, but the sleepless nights spent walking and calming a fussy baby were far more fun than those dealing with emergencies at the hospital.

Unfortunately, I didn't match into an orthopedic residency my first time. Orthopedics was a tough position and competition was fierce. In retrospect maybe it was for the best; I believe I'm too mild and mellow for such a specialty. The experience made me rethink my career choices and I opted not to try a second time for orthopedics. Instead, I decided to go back to the family practice residency I had originally planned.

After looking at the possibilities, I contacted the family practice residency director at the University of Cincinnati Medical Center, Dr. Andy Filak, whom I knew from my time in Cincinnati during medical school. He told me they would hold a spot for me the following year so I didn't need to go through the match program.

One of the benefits of family practice was that from the start I got an office in the Family Medicine Clinic in addition to my rotation through different specialties. MJ got a job at Christ Hospital in their nurse anesthesia program. During the three years of my family practice residency, MJ and I had two more children, Michael and Kristina.

Then MJ started disappearing again. Fortunately, she seemed to have a good sense of timing, mostly leaving when I was home and not on call for the weekend. Nonetheless, during this time she struggled a great deal, and I made sure I was actively involved in child care. That often meant coming home at noon for a quick visit to check up on everyone.

During my family practice residency, I returned to Millersburg to visit my family more often. Over time I became good friends with Dr. Roy Miller, who was actively recruiting me to join him in his practice. I took him up on his offer and we moved back to Millersburg in 1988.

In Millersburg, MJ took advantage of our increased family babysitting options to leave more often and stay away longer, a behavior that was simplified by her lack of a job. I was fortunate to arrange a babysitter, who was able to stay at our house for those last-minute escapes.

Once MJ came to me and said she was taking all the children down to visit her parents, who lived in Florida. She loaded up the car, and I kissed the kids goodbye and asked her to call me when she stopped along the way. She showed up at home again a few hours later in tears.

She put the kids in the living room, sobbing, "Here they

are, Bert. I can't take it."

She left again, alone, and didn't return for more than two weeks—the longest she was ever gone. She never said where she went. Her parents said she never showed up at their house. When she returned, though, she was calmer.

I confessed to my best friend Mike and his wife, Kathy, about the situation.

"Just know, Mike, if I'm ever found dead, it wasn't me. I would never commit suicide."

Those times were ominous and difficult for me. Life was always unstable with MJ. She often woke up at night with her eyes glazed over and glowing eerily. They didn't seem to focus on anything.

"Bert, I need to talk to you," she said. She would rant about something she was upset about. The next morning life would go on as if nothing had happened. The only problem was I lost even more sleep than usual.

On one of my on-call weekends, something even stranger happened. When on-call, I needed to be reachable by phone in case of emergencies, and if the phone call didn't reach me my pager beeped to let me know I needed to call the hospital back.

One night MJ and I had just gone upstairs to go to bed when the pager went off. I said, "That's odd. The phone didn't even ring." We didn't have a phone upstairs, so I went downstairs to the kitchen to call the hospital.

Where the phone normally hung on the wall I saw only an empty phone outlet. I went to the other phone in the study and found the desk bare. All the phones were gone.

"MJ, what did you do with the phones?"

I got no response. I knew she was still awake, although she hadn't said anything when I wondered out loud why the phone didn't ring.

I went back upstairs, sat on the bed, and said, "MJ, can you please tell me where the phones are? I need to call the hospital."

She refused to speak to me.

Talking only to the shadow of a being that had taken my wife's place, I said, "I guess I have to go to the hospital to see what they need, since I can't call them." I got dressed and went out the door.

I got all the way to the car. As I opened the car door, she came out and stood in the doorway.

"They're in the oven, Bert."

At first, I wasn't sure what she was talking about. I thought I had heard wrong. But when I went to look, inside the cold oven I found our two phones.

I got them out and put them back where they belonged. Then I finally called to check in on what the hospital needed.

————

My prospects for partnering with Dr. Roy Miller were quite positive. Salary in private practice was a big improvement over that as a resident.

MJ frequently brought the kids to my office and left them while she took off. I kept some toys on hand and the nursing staff helped care for the kids until my work was done for the day. Then I had to find a babysitter so I could work the next several days.

Dr. Roy Miller hated MJ and felt she was a poor partner for me. He told me, "She is the poorest excuse for a human being I have ever met." MJ hated Roy in equal proportion. Their mutual hostility created an untenable strain between me and Roy, to the point where we both felt that if I wanted to hold onto my marriage, it would be in both of our interests to look for another practice.

I started exploring my options and found Dr. John Robinson, who had decreased his practice considerably, was getting ready to close his office in Wooster, a small town twenty minutes away. I started working with him a few days a week to get to know his patients, telling them I was happy to take over their medical care when Dr. Robinson retired. We agreed that if they wanted to transition to a different physician, I would transfer their records. Nearly all his patients ended up staying with me.

Once he retired, I opened an office on the north side of town and started adding new patients as well. At first, I shared call with the two other physicians in the building, which meant we each only needed to be on call every third weekend. The practice grew rapidly and I soon hired a second nurse.

Later two more doctors joined the group. Our call schedule was every fifth weekend, making for a nice rotation. On Friday evenings each of us called whoever was on call that weekend to provide a summary of our patients who were in the hospital, along with information on any patients who might need attention over the weekend.

By now my practice had grown to about 2,000 active patients and it was nice to have some weekends free from phone calls. My youngest daughter, Sara, was born the first year we moved to Wooster. At the time my other children had chickenpox, so they were not allowed in the hospital. They were all so excited to see the new baby, it was hard to keep them away from her until they were no longer contagious.

IN THE ER

For as much as I seemed to have found my true calling as a doctor, my old way of life never stopped crossing my path. Working in the ER had a way of testing my ideals and beliefs.

The hospital I worked for was in Wayne County, Ohio, which includes an Amish community, and we frequently got farming and other accidents in the emergency room. Amish buggies had to travel on a major highway, resulting in occasional motor vehicle and buggy accidents.

One day a buggy carrying four children and their mother was struck by a large truck going at a high speed. One child was pronounced dead at the scene. Two children and the mother were critically injured. The other child was injured but could be treated at our facility. Our local Emergency Medical Services system dispatched helicopters to transport the critically injured patients from my hospital to a trauma center.

As the patients arrived in my emergency room, I recognized them as Old Order Amish by their clothing and knew they would not be happy about a helicopter ambulance ride. We rushed the first two children into helicopters and sent them on their way to Akron Children's Hospital. One of the helicopters was on its way back to pick up the mother when her husband arrived, followed within minutes by their Amish preacher. They wasted no time informing us that they did not allow helicopter transportation and made it clear how disappointed they were that we had already sent the two children off.

"It is part of our religion not to fly. We do not authorize you to send my wife by helicopter."

"Sir, she may die if we cannot get her the appropriate surgery fast. We're just a small local hospital and don't have the specialized equipment we need to save her life."

Despite our arguments, they refused to allow the flight. We canceled the helicopter and transported the mother to Akron General Medical Center by ambulance instead. I refused to feel guilty for sending the two children by air ambulance, as they could not speak for themselves and it was clearly in their best interest.

Many Amish believe it is better to risk their lives than to go against the rules of the church. Such beliefs can be hard for doctors who are attending patients, especially when we know we lack the resources to save someone who could easily be saved at the right facility.

Our preliminary x-rays, taken to diagnose the Amish woman for safe transfer to the trauma center, revealed a punctured lung. We inserted a chest tube to fix the lung, stabilizing her until the ambulance got her to the trauma center. She remained in total spine protection with a cervical collar and spine board for transport. Imaging at the trauma center revealed a cervical spine fracture that required surgery, along with multiple rib fractures.

Fortunately, everyone who arrived alive at the hospital survived, even the mother.

The hospital was familiar with these kinds of incidents with the Amish. We had an unwritten and unspoken policy to get the kids out as fast as possible when they needed additional treatment. They had not chosen the Amish lifestyle yet, even if their parents had.

————

Stories about ER medicine can seem amazing, perhaps even miraculous, but they happen all the time. Often instinct (or years of clinical experience) can be as important as the years of training.

A truck driver came into our small hospital and said he thought he was having a heart attack. His symptoms seemed to confirm his self-diagnosis, and we were set to transport him via helicopter to a larger hospital that was better equipped to deal with his condition than we were. Following protocol, I sent his EKG to the cardiologist.

He and I agreed that the EKG looked like a STEMI, an acute heart attack. We discussed the treatment plan, which included a clot-buster medication.

But something seemed not quite right to me. I wondered if the patient had a dissecting aneurysm, in which case the clot medication would be the wrong treatment—a death sentence, in fact. We couldn't positively rule out a dissecting aneurysm, and in the end, I called the receiving hospital and talked to the receiving doctor. I told him of my suspicions and explained why I didn't give the patient the medicine. I suggested that the patient get a CTA (Cat Scan Angiogram) upon arrival before going to the heart cath suite.

About an hour later I got a call from the receiving doctor.

"Hi, Dr. Miller. I wanted to update you on the patient. As you had suspected, your patient did not have a heart attack. He had a thoracic aortic aneurysm. He went directly to the OR (operating room) following his CAT scan."

Following my instincts saved this patient's life.

About two months later that same patient stopped back in my emergency room while I was on duty. This time he was not sick and wore a big smile on his face.

"Dr. Miller, I wanted to thank you for making the right call and saving my life. I'm back driving my truck and extremely happy. I owe that to you."

Perhaps my most famous emergency medical story also involved a heart attack, a few years later. The Studer Group, an organization that helps hospitals improve patient satisfaction through targeted surveys, published a book titled *What is Right in Health Care.*

The administrator of the hospital I was working at in Alabama noticed my name in one of the case studies and called me over to talk. "Bert, did you work at Mercy Hospital in Willard, Ohio?"

"Sure, I worked there. Why?"

"Looks like you made one of the case studies in this book," he said, handing me the article to read.

It described a case I remembered well. Mercy Hospital had actually used the patient in commercials, even on billboards. A firefighter trained in first response came to the ER because he had been mowing the lawn and felt signs of a heart attack. As a medic, he knew these symptoms well. I was at my desk and saw him walk in, escorted by a nurse.

The patient appeared pale and wet with sweat. That was all I needed to see to know he was in trouble. We rushed to hook him up to the heart monitors and get an EKG and IV.

He looked at me and said, "I think I'm having a heart attack."

As the EKG printed out, I said, "I think you're right. The EKG shows a STEMI."

I reminded him that things would happen fast now. My team all worked together to prep him for the helicopter to take him to a larger hospital that could do a heart catheter and stent placement.

"Doc, am I going to die?" he asked.

I looked him square in the face and said, "That's not in our plans, sir."

A few minutes later he went into cardiac arrest. We initiated

CPR, injected some medicines in his IV, and shocked his heart twice before it returned to a normal rhythm. We got him stabilized and sent him by Flight for Life to the Toledo hospital, where they inserted a stent. He recovered with completely normal cardiac function.

Later, he came back to thank me for being so candid, supportive, and honest. He said that my words were the last thing he remembered before waking up in the hospital in Toledo.

DIVORCE

When MJ and I got married, everything about our relationship seemed to change. I now seemed to be the target of her mood swings. When she was in one of her moods, nothing I did was ever right. She intentionally gave me impossible tasks. She wanted me to make money for the family but also wanted me at home. She wanted alone time, but then was angry when she got it. She could change moods in a flash. One minute I was the worst person in the world and she was berating me then the next moment everything was fine. That kind of discontinuity was hard to take over and over again.

Even without medical school, I could have recognized the signs: MJ clearly had mental issues. Yet she had an amazing ability to turn it on and off. On several different occasions,

I convinced her to see a psychologist with me, starting when we lived in Cincinnati. She soon got disappointed with the counselor and quit the sessions. We tried a different counselor and the same thing happened. When we moved to Wooster, I again convinced her to see a couples counselor. In addition to our joint sessions, I went alone to seek help in coping with her problems. The counselor told me that MJ was not likely to change and I had to decide whether I could live with her behavior. I needed to consider what effect it had on the children.

I believe that MJ never thought I would file for divorce because of my Amish background and belief system. Initially, she was right. I had chosen to marry her for better or worse, and I believed it was my duty to stick it out. I knew divorce would be a hard pill to swallow for my parents and Amish relatives, and I kept hoping that counseling would help her change her behavior.

I thought about divorce on numerous occasions. MJ had issues, I knew; she'd had them when I married her. Deep down I feared divorce would be worse for the kids than leaving the kids in her care. But as time went on and her behavior only worsened, I decided the environment was not appropriate for our children. It took six years, but I finally realized I couldn't help her. I had to ask myself, *Is this the kind of life I really want my kids to think is normal?*

Is it better to stay married to avoid the stigma of divorce? To stay together and have the children accept her strange behavior as normal?

Will the children grow up to have similar dysfunctional relationships?

Divorce was not a spur-of-the-moment decision for me. At the time divorce still had an extremely negative stigma and wasn't common, especially in small towns. I talked to a lot of our mutual friends and family. My brother John and his wife, Esther, knew of the problems, though not in detail. He was the brother I remained closest with. I rarely talked about these issues with my parents, but they knew sometimes I needed a babysitter at a moment's notice.

It was easier to discuss the idea of divorce with my in-laws than with my own family. In the end, my mother-in-law was the one who convinced me divorce was the best option. She said, "Bert, we know things are not good. If you feel you need to get a divorce, then you need to just do it. You have to look out for those kids."

Shortly after this conversation, another incident provided the final straw.

Before Michael started grade school, I knew MJ was having one of her difficult times. I told Michael and MJ that he could spend the day with me at the office as I saw patients. The plan was that I would pick Michael up after my morning rounds at the hospital and take him with me to the office. I felt this would lighten the load for MJ. While I was at the hospital, she called me.

"Bert, don't come pick up Michael. He's not behaving, so he doesn't get to go with you to the office ."

"What's he doing?"

"He won't listen to me or do what he's supposed to do."

"Hmm. I understand. Could I talk to Michael?"

She handed the phone to our son.

He sobbed, "Dad, I just don't know what she wants me to do . . . *hmm sniffle*. She tells me to fold the laundry and then tells me to watch the baby . . . *hmm sniffle* . . . I can't do it all at the same time. I just don't know what to do . . . *sob*."

John and Esther were the first in the Amish community I told.

John said, "Well, Bert, you know what is best. But no matter how difficult it will be, you have to talk to Datt about this."

I tried to picture how that conversation would go.

"Datt, I've had to make a difficult decision. I'm filing for divorce from MJ. I've tried my best and have been thinking about it for a while now. She refuses to get help and her mood swings have become overwhelming. I really don't want to do this, but I truly feel it is best for the children that we separate. I'm afraid that my relationship with MJ, with all the constant disruptions and unpredictability, is sending the wrong message to our children. I don't want them to think that this is normal."

I didn't want my datt to think I had failed. I didn't want to be talked out of it, either. I needed support and was sure I wouldn't get that from him. I ran the scenario through my head a million times, but I delayed telling him until I had the conviction to follow through.

———

When I finally got up the courage to file for divorce, I fully expected to get custody of my kids. I had been the most stable parent and had tried to protect them from their mother's mood swings. I was their sole parent during MJ's frequent extended absences. The court system didn't see it that way, but I didn't know that until it was too late.

MJ took the divorce filing as an act of war. She did everything in her power, even made things up, in an attempt to get me to give up my visitation rights and move on with my life without my children.

One of the hardest things about the process was that although most of our mutual friends—even the Nofzigers and the Lekans—knew MJ was a little bit crazy, they sided with her. They wouldn't talk to me, even though I thought they knew what was going on and what she was doing. After a long time, they started to understand the situation. I didn't fight for those relationships, even though losing them made me sad. I knew that MJ needed their support more than I did.

This was a very difficult time in my life. The divorce process was full of conflict. MJ and her attorney dragged the proceedings out as long as they could, making everything as difficult as possible. She fought me tooth and nail, from the day I first filed until the day my youngest daughter moved out of her house almost ten years later.

I kept telling myself, *someday the kids will see*. I tried not to be biased or turn my kids against their mother. To address conflicts I always said, "I'm sorry your mom feels that way, but that's not what happened."

I thought I would get full custody of the children because I truly believed MJ didn't want it, but the Wayne County Court system, like much of small-town America, was skewed in favor of the mother.

Despite the fact that I was the parent who provided most of the care, my request for full custody was denied. The judge decided shared custody was the better option. My lawyer was unable to convince him that the children would be best served in my custody. How MJ's erratic behavior didn't register with the judge was beyond my understanding. I thought some of the outrageous things she did would have backfired on her, but nothing seemed to sway the judge from the belief that "mother knows best."

The judge ruled in favor of shared custody with MJ as the residential parent. The kids got to spend every other weekend at my house, along with every Wednesday for a few hours at suppertime.

My lawyer said, "We could appeal it, but the odds are it won't change the outcome. You are in Wayne County, and unless the mother has had some major issues recorded, she always gets primary custody. The fact that you have shared custody is unusual here." I chose not to appeal the decision.

I called my mother- and father-in-law to tell them the bad news. After the divorce, I kept in contact with them. I even took the kids to visit them until one day my mother-in-law said, "Bert, I need to tell you something. And, well, you know MJ well enough to know this, but we need to stop communicating with you. MJ said if we have any known, active dialogue with you, she won't let us see the kids anymore. You are welcome to stop by whenever you want. Our door is always open and we won't turn you away. But we can't invite you. And we have to limit our conversations. I'm so sorry, Bert."

While it hurt me to lose people who had supported me through this difficult time, I knew it was true. MJ hadn't let her parents even see Sara until she was almost six months old, even though they had asked repeatedly, just because she was upset about something.

MJ had always brought the kids to the office and left them with me when she lost patience and was fed up with them. She handed me the diaper bag and some Cheerios and said, "Here they are. I can't take it anymore," then turned and walked out. I would settle the kids in with their snacks and toys, finish seeing patients, and then find a babysitter.

I assumed that after all the legal conflicts were settled, she would continue that pattern, however, she never did.

———

After the divorce, MJ did one irrational thing after another. She wouldn't pull into the driveway to pick up or drop off the kids; she parked at the end of the driveway on the road. When the children returned to her house, they couldn't wear the clothes I bought them; she kept those in a bag in the closet and only allowed the kids to wear them when they visited me.

Once she tried to file domestic violence charges against me. At Mike and Elizabeth's T-ball game, a big storm was brewing, potentially a tornado, and the game had been called off. An announcement had been made for everyone to get home as quickly as possible. I went to MJ's car to get the kids' things and put Mike's cleats in her car. As I reached into the car, MJ appeared. Perhaps she thought I was getting in the car, even though my only thought was to get the kids to safety. She huffed and sort of danced around. I didn't know what she was doing until she suddenly poured her soda on me and screamed, "You saw it! You saw it! He hit me!"

Absolutely nothing had happened, except that I was now soaked and sticky with Diet Coke. She made a huge scene and later, unknown to me, filed a police report and talked to the county prosecutor. She claimed that I had abused her. I was devastated. Not only was it a lie, but it was also a lie that could cost me my medical license.

MJ was out to hurt me as much as possible. We went to court over every little thing, real or imagined. I thought the family court judge might have figured out her game. When she couldn't remember a lie she had made up in court, she simply refused to answer questions. After a while, the judge would say, "I'll use your previous answer in response then unless you tell me differently." My lawyer suggested an attorney from Akron represent me during the domestic violence trial and proceedings. The county prosecutor at the criminal trial was a woman, and I prepared myself for the same bias I saw in the divorce cases: the mother was always right.

MJ was determined to punish me as much as possible. It was obvious to me that she had made up the abuse to get back at me over the divorce. The incident might have been funny if both my livelihood and my relationship with my children weren't hanging in the balance.

In general, prosecutors, even if they don't think the defendant is guilty, want to win their case. However, after listening to my testimony, the family court prosecutor— whose job it was to find me guilty—seemed to change her strategy. She didn't stop prosecuting, but she dropped her aggressive attitude toward me. She almost seemed on my side in her prosecution, as if she no longer believed I was guilty. She asked, "Did anyone hit anyone?"

"No, MJ poured Diet Coke on me. But she didn't hit me, and I didn't hit her."

"When this happened, how close were you to Mary Jane?'

"Can I show you/"

The judge nodded approval.

"I was getting Mike's shoes out of the car like this. Before I knew it, Diet Coke was all over me, and MJ was screaming, right about where you are," I said.

The case went on to final arguments and the jury filed out to deliberate. My attorney and I stepped outside, and he lit up a cigarette. He barely had time for a few puffs before the bailiff came back and said the jury had reached their decision.

My lawyer raised his hand in a salute of victory. "All right!"

"How do you know what the verdict is?"

"No jury convicts someone in under five minutes. You've

been found innocent."

After the not guilty verdict was read, every single juror came over to shake my hand. In various manners, they said they were sorry I had to go through that experience.

Defeat didn't bother MJ. She brought charge after trumped-up charge to family court, year after year for ten years. I had the sense that she was simply trying to wear me down, to the point where I would leave town and not be a part of the children's lives. Although the strain was difficult, the father in me could never leave my children behind. I knew the day would come when my kids needed me, and it did.

MJ continued to use the children as a weapon against me until, once they reached the age of twelve years, when Wayne County let them choose their custodial parent, they each came to live with me. She didn't fight for them then, as she knew this was going to be each child's decision. She didn't even want the parental visitations that were given to her every Wednesday evening and every other weekend. Once the children came to live with me, I was the sole parental figure in their lives again, she stepped away - this time for good.

A DAUGHTER'S CHOICE

We went to court every year that I can remember from when I was seven until I turned eighteen.

Over a decade of judges hearing one thing after another from my mother with limited to no proof.

We went because my ears got sunburnt, she claimed it was child abuse.

We went over money, she needed more.

We went overtime off and changed dates. Suddenly she forgot that doctors' schedules and court times don't always correlate.

We went for anything my mom could imagine. Most of the time we weren't even sure why we were going. We were just shuffled in the car and told to tell the truth, but a very specific truth.

We were forced to go to psychologists who twisted our words as they handed us a teddy bear to hug and share our feelings with. Anything you shared would be twisted and turned into something different by adults. The truth was questioned so many times or called a lie so often that you weren't really sure what either of those words meant to anyone. It didn't take long to learn it was better not to share anything or someone got hurt - usually me somehow.

It's hard to know as a kid what is right and what is wrong when everyone tells you something different. You hear one thing, then you see people do another. When nothing is stable, how do you decide where to build your foundation?

Slowly, as I started to spend time in friends' homes, I realized that some things that were completely normal in my life weren't normal. I started to re-evaluate my opinions. I had taken care of my siblings for as long as

I could remember, cooking dinner while standing on a chair when Mom didn't show up for whatever reason and helping them. I had never considered that other mothers might not require that of their eldest child.

The worst part about court was I had to choose which parent to live with by myself. My siblings couldn't come with me. So for me, it wasn't a matter of choosing the best parent but having to make a sacrifice by abandoning three children to something the judge continued to deem as 'fit' to test if there really was a better situation out there for us.

After much questioning, consideration, and fear, I choose to leave and live with my Dad. It was a gamble. All I ever knew of life was that it was not how it appeared from the outside. It meant leaving my siblings who I had helped raise since I was a little kid. It meant a lot of risk and responsibility built around one decision on the shoulders of a twelve-year-old.

My mother allowed me to pack all my things but refused to let me take more than the clothes on my back. I never saw the rest of my belongings and wasn't allowed to see my brothers and sisters or even call them. Essentially, I was shunned from the life I'd known with my mother. My younger siblings didn't understand and obviously felt abandoned. My mother fed that myth.

In the end, my choice helped to pave the way for each of them to move over and live with my Dad which, while not perfect, in the end, was the more stable of the two homes, and a better environment.

TRANSITIONS

As Amish children, we did not visit the doctor very often. My dad had a book of medicinal remedies and relied on old-time treatments to handle common ailments.

The Common Cold: My memm put peppermint oil in water boiling on the stove and we leaned over to inhale the steam to clear our sinuses. Memm also rubbed Vicks Vapo-rub on our chest to ease congestion.

Earache: When we complained of ear pains, my dad smoked a cigar and then blew smoke in our ears, and put a warm towel over it. I remember the treatment feeling very comforting, although today, I have doubts about how medically effective it was.

Boils: Freshly cut raw onions placed on a boil helped bring it to a head so it could be popped and the pus could drain.

Disinfecting: Kerosene was used to clean and disinfect wounds.

Burns: Memm rubbed cool butter on burns to help relieve the fire on the skin and provide moisture.

The list of home remedies went on and on. While I wondered about their efficacy, as a doctor I was a strong proponent of vitamins and supplements use in my practice. I still believe that eating well and using vitamins and supplements can prevent a lot of illnesses. In my practice, I encouraged natural remedies rather than drugs whenever appropriate.

In the early 1990s insurance companies and pharmaceutical companies strongly pushed a number of medications that I did not feel were appropriate, with the number-one example being cholesterol medication. To meet the standard of care, I was expected to treat every patient whose cholesterol was over two hundred, despite the lack of evidence that treating the general population to lower their cholesterol actually helped in reducing the incidence of heart disease and stroke. Strong evidence supported using these medications to help prevent second heart attacks and second strokes, but not as much prior to an initial episode. At the same time, proven evidence showed a significant number of side effects from these medications.

As a result, I started shifting the focus of my practice toward alternative medicines and attending conferences on age-management medicine.

MJ and I had been divorced by this time, which meant if I was on call when the kids were at my house I needed a babysitter on standby. Limiting my practice to age management allowed me to build a schedule that didn't require me to be on call. The time I had with my kids I could actually spend with them instead of leaving them with someone else.

I gradually phased out my traditional family practice in the mid-1990s. To replace the income lost from family practice, I started working more in the emergency room. In addition, I added aesthetic procedures such as laser hair removal and aesthetic treatments to my practice.

The more I worked in the emergency room, the more I loved it. The unpredictability of what came through the door next rejuvenated my excitement for medicine. It wasn't long before I was working full-time in emergency medicine and only part-time in my office. I had an aesthetician and two additional employees who handled some of the procedures to keep the office afloat when I wasn't there.

A SECOND MARRIAGE

Despite moving on from my conservative upbringing, I never thought about dating after a divorce. I hadn't ever imagined getting divorced, plus I hadn't been particularly skilled at dating before I got married.

Nevertheless, I went on a number of dates, mostly with women I met through work or who were introduced by friends. A number of these first dates were last dates. I only went out with three people I liked enough to have a follow-up date with. One of those was Pat.

I first went out with Pat on a blind double date. The setup was somewhat awkward: a friend, Dr. Alan Gatz, and his wife, Barb, had met Pat when she came to hang wallpaper in their office and had mentioned me to her. They thought we would be a good match.

We arranged for the four of us to go out for pizza. Although the group planned to meet there, I called Pat beforehand. I decided I should pick her up and treat it like a real date, hoping that would help make dinner less awkward. After pizza the four of us went back to my house for ice cream and card games. I had a great time despite my reservations about getting into a relationship again. I wasn't dating a lot at the time so I wasn't in any hurry to schedule a second date. Despite Alan encouraging me to call Pat again, a month passed. I just wasn't convinced I was ready for anything to move forward, so I didn't make it a priority.

About a month later, I was supposed to spend Valentine's Day weekend with my kids, but yet again their mom made it impossible. At the last minute, I called Pat instead.

The second date felt equally awkward at first, especially since we hadn't spoken since our first date, and I had called her purely on impulse. I didn't want to show up empty-handed, especially on Valentine's Day weekend, so I stopped at the local grocery store and bought a heart-shaped vase with a rose in it.

Instead of going out to a restaurant in the Valentine's day rush, we stayed home for snacks and a few drinks. We spent the whole evening talking and watching TV. Pat was so easy to talk to, and it felt great to have someone actually listen to my conversation for a change. From then on we dated regularly. She did thoughtful things like going to my house to do my laundry and leaving a spritz of her perfume on my pillow when I was at work. The realization that she had been in my house made me happy to come home.

It wasn't long before we were a true partnership and talking about getting married. Pat had two children from her first marriage. To help prepare them for such a big change, we started getting all six of our kids together for activities so they could get to know each other.

One of our major considerations was where to live—a place big enough to hold eight people when the whole family was together. One day Pat and I spotted a *FOR SALE* sign in a yard and stopped to look around. The back door was unlocked, so we gave ourselves a tour. The house needed a lot of work both inside and out, but it had potential!

After contacting the realtor, we bought the house. Step by step we renovated and fixed it up to suit our needs. Gradually my children moved in and joined us until it felt like home to me again. It proved to be a great place for us to spend time with our kids. We spent sixteen happy years in that house while the children grew up and went on to college and then Pat and I moved to Dothan, Alabama.

————

Second marriages always come with their own trials and tribulations. Pat already knew about my issues with MJ. We came into the relationship knowing we had to juggle a blended family of eight people, plus ex-spouses and all the drama that comes with divorce. That made for some interesting adventures.

Though we didn't have a large wedding, we had fun planning it. We wanted all the children to feel like they were a part of the day, but we also expected that MJ would try to sabotage our plans. Full of the hope of soon-to-be-newlyweds, we made sure that the children all had their special wedding outfits, although we kept them at our house. We knew MJ would never allow my children to take them to her house.

The plan for the day of the wedding was to pick my children up and have them get dressed at our house. MJ had agreed to let us have the kids even though it wasn't my usual day with them.

The morning of the wedding, my oldest daughter called. "Hi Daddy," she whispered.

"Hi, Elizabeth. How are you, honey?"

"Mom is making us go to the library today."

"That's fine. Should we pick you up after that?"

There was a long pause on the line. "I don't think so. I'm sorry, Daddy."

Click. The line disconnected.

MJ didn't let her give me any details. Still, we went to the house at the appointed time, hoping that maybe something had changed. No one answered the doorbell. The house was empty.

I knew then my children wouldn't be at the wedding. Though Pat and I were both disappointed, neither of us was really surprised. If MJ wanted to let the kids attend, she wouldn't have taken them to the library, and she wouldn't have let Elizabeth call to tell me about it unless she wanted a scene. Some things simply weren't worth arguing about with her. Besides, recalling what had happened at the baseball field, I knew that if I made any attempt to pick up the kids in a public space, a huge confrontation would erupt and ruin our big day. I was sure that was what she hoped for. I refused to give her that satisfaction.

At the wedding, their presence was sorely missed. At the reception, I said, "Obviously, we have some empty seats here today. And we sure wish everyone could have been here with us to celebrate. Unfortunately, some things are just beyond our control."

The kids were sad about not getting to wear their wedding clothes, and I knew they felt bad about missing the ceremony, but we let them know it wasn't their fault.

I didn't anticipate that any of my Amish relatives would come to my second wedding, especially considering none had come to the first wedding. I had invited John and Esther but told them I understood if they weren't comfortable attending. It was one thing to talk to me; I knew it was something else for them to openly support a second marriage. It was no surprise to me when they didn't show up either. Once again I relied on friends to fill in where family wouldn't.

PAT AND THE AMISH

Amish gatherings, even among close family, tend to have long periods of silence between bouts of talking.

Communal silence, when no one is eating or talking, is common. While for the Amish such extended silence is natural, it can be uncomfortable for others. It took Pat a while to get used to it.

The first Amish relatives that Pat met were, naturally, my brother John and his family. It must have been awkward for her to meet them, but she liked their kids and quickly felt at home with them compared to my other relatives. They were friendly and quickly accepted Pat and our marriage.

Pat always considered John and Esther the easiest of my family to get along with. Esther and Pat often traded tips on gardening and herbs. Pat always felt like she was one of the English people they could ask for information without her being judgmental. Her favorite thing was when they came to our house to visit. Then Esther asked about the washing machine, dishwasher, and other English conveniences, and sometimes they traded recipes. With John and Esther, Pat felt at home. Not quite the same when we went to visit my parents.

Meeting my parents was a different ball game. By this time my memm was already suffering from poor health and mild dementia, so she didn't cause much of an issue. As expected, my datt did not make it easy on my new wife.

The only time a visit to my parents was fun—or rather, funny—was not a pleasant experience for Pat. We had been down to see them a number of times, and Pat was starting to feel a little more comfortable. As we were getting ready to say our goodbyes, she went to hug my sister, Esther, who lived with my parents to care for them. Both of us still remember how Esther tensed up as if she were being attacked.

Hugs and similar displays of personal affection in front of others are rare among the Amish, generally reserved for children. Adults usually greet each other with a handshake or just a nod, but I had forgotten to mention this point to Pat. To her, hugging family members was perfectly natural. That's what her family and our children all did. Hugs are an English characteristic of family life, and I'd gotten so used to them I had forgotten the cultural difference.

Frozen in an awkward hug, Pat realized she'd made a mistake. She learned, quickly and abruptly, that my parents were inflexible. I knew Pat often wished she didn't have to go to their house; she went to support me. If it wasn't fun for me, it was worse for her. The Amish weren't the wholesome community she had imagined. She was shocked by so many unexpected aspects—the treatment of farm animals, the unrestrained dog breeding conditions, and the overall coldness.

She also knew the Amish didn't believe in divorce and second marriages. I tried my best to make sure she was respected, but my family still did annoying things like not including her on invitations to weddings and family events and often spoke Pennsylvania Dutch in her presence. In no uncertain terms, I told them that if Pat wasn't invited and welcomed, I wouldn't attend. It took time to break down those barriers, but now Pat is allowed to sit with me at events, which helps her feel more comfortable around my family.

Pat told me, "My expectation of the Amish, from when

I've seen them on TV or read about them, is that they seem homey. Almost like they are warm and cuddly, accepting of people, but that's not the case. Your dad is cold and really doesn't even acknowledge I'm there. Your mom of course isn't well so that's understandable for her. Visiting them isn't something I ever look forward to. Maybe if we could spend some time with the horses and the other animals it would be more enjoyable."

FLYING BLIND

Once Pat and I went to Amelia Island, in my single-engine airplane, one of the Florida barrier islands near Jacksonville, for a brief getaway trip. I had never flown into the Amelia Island airport. We stopped to refuel our 4-place Mooney in Charleston, South Carolina, under clear skies but ran into some scattered clouds that quickly condensed into a thick layer of clouds with no visual ground contact.

I had filed my flight plan with the flight control center and had clearance to fly a pre-set path to the airport. I kept in constant radio contact with the control center as they followed my plane on their radar to ensure no other planes came near us when we were in the clouds.

As we got close to Amelia Island airport, the control center transferred us to the approach control, which directs planes on their final approach.

When I reported to the approach air traffic controller, he identified my aircraft on his radar and gave the usual response of "61 Whiskey, radar contact."

Next, I heard "61 Whiskey, no direct weather report available. Automated weather for a report is available on 122.3. The last two aircraft missed the approach. I show the airport fifteen miles at 2:00. What are your intentions?" The last two planes had been unable to identify the runway as they descended through the clouds to the minimum altitude allowed by their approach.

I had already listened to the automated weather report, which reported clouds with a ceiling at 800 feet. Based on that information, I said I wanted to try the approach.

The controller instructed, "61 Whiskey, descend to 3,000 feet, fly heading 200 vectors to ILS13 approach" to help me line up with the runway. I was expected to land the airplane if I saw the runway, or if not, I had to execute a missed approach by climbing in the direction of my pre-set flight approach. Then I needed to recontact the controller either to make another pass or receive clearance to another airport. Before I could respond, the airplane lost all electrical power.

Without power, I had no navigation or directional instruments and no radio communication with the tower. My altimeter, airspeed indicator, and turn indicator still worked off airflow. Luckily, I also had a small battery-powered GPS that I always carried as a backup. Surrounded by clouds and using the simplest of tools, Pat and I found a hole in the clouds. Flying an airplane has a lot to do with faith and a sense of direction. These are two characteristics I'd worked a lifetime to fine-tune, so I was able to stay calm despite the uncertainty and stress.

I decided to descend through the hole in a spiraling turn, dropping to 1,000 feet above the ground. Clouds were still all around us. Uncomfortable descending lower without any visibility, I climbed back up.

I remembered Pat Kissel, my flight instructor's words: "Bert, never start anything until you know how you are going to finish it." The charted ILS approach into Amelia Island airport allowed me to descend down to 400 feet. I decided my last good option to get into the tiny airport was to use my handheld GPS to direct me on my original approach, descending to 200 feet.

I told Pat my plan so she could brace herself for our next steps. "If I don't see the runway at 200 feet, we have no choice but to execute a missed approach and climb back above the clouds. Our only chance without instruments would be to find a hole in the clouds somewhere with an airport nearby." "Ok, I trust you," she said, although she didn't look especially confident.

As we dropped down to 400 feet we were still in the clouds, but I caught glimpses of the ground below. At just a quarter-mile from the airport I kept my altitude 400 feet, I eased back on the power as the GPS indicated the plane was approaching the beginning of the runway.

"Bert, I think I see a number 13," Pat said.

"Great!" I pulled back. We were able to line up visually in those last few feet between the clouds and the ground for a nice smooth landing.

Down on the ground, the base operator greeted us on the ramp. "Someone will surely be happy to hear from you. The Savannah control tower is anxious to talk to you," he said.

I called the control tower and told them we had landed safely. The controller said they were concerned because as we spiraled down to try for a visual landing, we dropped off their radar. Then a plane appeared, almost in the same spot, maneuvering to an approach landing. They were fairly sure it was our airplane but couldn't verify that without communication. As a backup option, the tower had two military F-16s ready to take off to assist us.

"How would the F-16s have helped me? I fly a lot slower than they do."

He said, "The pilots would have used hand signals to direct you where to fly to get to another runway." The F-16s would have taken turns flying next to my plane, staying as long as possible until I could land safely.

Our instruments going offline had created quite a commotion! Pat and I celebrated our successful return to Earth with a fine dinner at the best restaurant we could find on the island.

YOU CAN'T DO THAT!

RECONCILIATION AND DEATH

One morning I was on my way to Willard Hospital for a 24-hour shift when I got a phone call.

"Albert, it's your brother John. You know Memm has been really sick, and we want you to come home. Mose told me to call and invite you. We are doing her last rites ceremony tonight."

I asked John about my mother's condition and he updated me on the family gossip before I broached the question I really wanted to ask.

"John, I need to ask you something. Did Mose ask you to tell me about Memm's last rites, or did he actually ask you to invite me?" I wanted to be sure the family wanted me there and didn't just want to make me feel guilty for not showing up.

John chuckled. He knew how hard my family could be on me and was used to being the go-between. Through all my family issues, John has always been my one true brotherly friend and family member.

"I know what you mean, Albert, so I asked him specifically what he meant before I called. What he said exactly was, 'We want Albert to know he is invited and we would like him to come.'"

"It's been a long time since I was invited to something important and not just told about it after the fact. But I'm sorry, John I can't get anyone to cover my shift so last-minute, and I can't leave the hospital in the lurch. I'll come tomorrow as soon as I get off work."

The next day I went to see my mother, the last time I talked with her. It was a pleasant visit although she was in her last hours of life. Her voice was very weak, and she drifted in and out of sleep. Whenever she woke, she repeatedly asked if I was still there. She kept thanking me for coming.

Memm passed away on May 18, 2004, at 83 years old.

Pat and I went down for my memm's funeral and were both allowed to sit with my brothers and sisters. At previous funerals I had sat with non-family members, so sitting with the family, being acknowledged as a family member, was a welcome change.

Later I was called for the reading of my memm's will. "I bequeath my belongings to my husband in the event he is still alive upon my death. Upon his death, my belongings should be divided up among the children in equal proportions, except for Albert. Albert should get a one-half portion, compared to the other children."

After the reading, my datt said that he wanted to give some money to each of us from the will. He gave everyone a check that night. When he came to me, he paused before handing me an envelope. "Albert, I hope this is OK. I'm sorry, but yours is smaller than the others."

"Datt, you don't need to apologize. You have the right to do whatever you want with what you have. Anything is already more than I was expecting."

Toward the end of my memm and datt's lives, some

meaningful changes occurred. I started to be included more often, receiving invitations to weddings and other family events, not just funerals. In death, coming together to mourn seems to help the Amish set their differences aside.

Amish funerals are long, usually lasting three to four hours, without any of the hugging or hand-holding so typical of English funerals. At an appointed time, guests go through a receiving line to shake all the surviving family members' hands. The handshake is almost as dead as the corpse, limp with almost no grip. Then everyone walks past the body. People often touch the corpse in a last farewell.

Once everyone has filed through to see the body, the casket may be taken to another room for family members to have a more personal and private time of mourning full of tears, as people sit or stand around the casket. The extensive amount of crying, so different from the Amish's usual stoic emotional state, seems out of character.

In the end, some of the men screw the lid onto the coffin and then place the casket on a horse-drawn buggy. A slow procession of relatives and friends trails behind the buggy to the burial ground, usually a nearby family plot.

The graves are dug by hand the day before with a shovel, and despite the lack of technology, they are always perfectly rectangular with the side walls amazingly straight and smooth. The casket is slowly lowered to the bottom of the grave, as people standing around the grave sing Amish hymns. The singing continues as pallbearers take turns putting shovels of dirt on top of the casket until the grave is

PART 4. Science, Faith and Grace

refilled. Only after the dirt is tamped down does the crowd slowly dissipate.

———

Datt was weakened and sick for the final few years of his life. He was in his 90s when age and time finally started to take their toll on his will. Quite a few times my siblings thought he was on his deathbed, but he kept living as proof of his stubbornness. I believe he wanted to do something that took him years to work up the courage to actually do.

Even when facing death—or perhaps especially then—people cling to their choices because those determine their entire outlook on life. Even more so when they realize that some of their choices might have been better done another way.

Not long before my datt died, I went to see him.

"Albert, I know your memm and I didn't always treat you the way we should have. I hope you understand why we had to do it, I wouldn't do it that way if I had the to do it over again…" .

In so many words, he finally acknowledged that they hadn't always treated me right.

Datt saying those words out loud meant the world to me. I had longed to hear them for so long. After all the hurtful things that had been said over the years, I believe it was a healing experience for both of us; I know it was for me. It was the last real conversation we had before he passed.

After I left that day, my father told Mose, "Albert and I

241

made peace." A few days later, on December 10, 2012, he woke up and said to Mose, "Today I'm going to die."

I know he died with one less weight on his chest, his soul lightened with forgiveness. He was ninety-two years old.

Some people seem shocked that people know so accurately when they're about to die. They may think those who say that have chosen to give up on life. Yet as a doctor I'm not surprised by such knowledge. Many people are in tune with their bodies and recognize the signs. They know when it is time once they have done all the last things they needed to do, and are ready to face death with open arms. My father was a strong and spiritual man, and I have no doubt he knew what he was talking about.

As a doctor, I am used to talking about death. It's a natural part of life. I have seen powerful moments of patients meeting death with acceptance and dignity, here are a few examples.

One patient talked with family and friends as the last rites were performed. When the rituals were over, everyone said their goodbyes. His wife was the last one. When she leaned over and kissed him, he said, "I love you," as if he knew he was at the end and stopped breathing. I wasn't with him when he died; I had given him a physical exam about two hours earlier. The nurse on duty at the time witnessed his passing and shared the experience with me.

Another patient of mine was at the end of his life, suffering numerous conditions—lung cancer, chronic obstructive pulmonary disease (COPD), and congestive heart failure. He was ready for the end and no longer wanted to pursue any life-prolonging treatments. He asked me if I would go over his medications and tell him which ones prolonged life versus which were given for comfort. He wanted to understand what he could choose to quit and what he should continue.

I asked, "You understand that stopping this medicine will speed up death, right? Are you sure you're ready for that? Are you sure you only want to take medications to relieve your symptoms?"

"Dr. Miller, I'm as ready as I can be. My wife is taken care of, and if I had good health I'd be happy to live another ten years. But I'm ready to quit now. I'm in too much pain. I just can't function the way I used to. When I stop this medicine, how long will I have?"

"That's up to you and the man upstairs. No one knows for sure."

He nodded in response. That night he died in his sleep.

I think people can say, "Here, I am ready," and greet death like a friend as they let go of their life on Earth. The people that I have seen pass on this way seem to have made peace with those close to them, have a good relationship with God, and view death as a transition into eternal life.

LEAVING HOME

Most of my private practice was cash-based, not insurance-based. As I spent more time doing emergency medicine and less time at the office, I paid less attention to the office budget. Then something set off an alarm, and when I took a closer look I saw a disturbing trend. My practice was spending more money on supplies than we received from the sale of these items. An analysis revealed that my staff, whom I had trusted, was pocketing some of the cash sales and stealing from me. I was shocked and troubled.

My wife and I had already discussed the idea of moving south once the kids graduated from high school. This unsettling news made the decision easier; I closed my office in 2008. I chose not to pursue any legal action against any of my employees and fired only one, although I was never really sure who was involved in the theft.

Pat and I wanted to escape the cold Ohio winters. As a child, I had enjoyed playing in the snow, but as I got older I disliked the winter season more and more. A new home in a warm, small-to-medium size town with an easy drive to a beach sounded ideal.

Wooster was full of memories, some wonderful and some not so good. We wanted a clean start to live out our time together, leaving behind the baggage of our previous lives.

When our youngest daughter, Sara, was in her last year of high school, we started to look at options and found a place in southeastern Alabama—just an hour and a half from the beach, but inland enough that we didn't have to worry about hurricanes. We saw it with starry eyes—not realizing the area was prone to tornadoes and other foul weather.

An offer from Dale Medical Center in Ozark, Alabama, for a position as an ER doctor, arrived at the perfect time. For the first year, I continued to work part-time, spending one week of each month in Ohio until we sold our house and made the move permanent.

We bought a home in Dothan, Alabama, and as time passed I started working part-time at Flowers Hospital ER as well. Eventually, an ER staffing company that I had worked for in Ohio took over Flowers Hospital's ER physician staffing, and I went to work for them full time.

Pat and I have since lived happily here in Dothan for the past twelve years. We joined the Covenant United Methodist Church in Dothan and have been active in church activities, including mission trips to Panama. We enjoy entertaining, fine dining and wine, going to the beach with friends, and attending church events.

In our free time, Pat and I visit our children scattered around the globe, from Ohio to Florida to Colorado and as far away as Brazil.

A DAUGHTER'S PATH

The challenge of trying to assimilate where you 'should be' a local completely resonates with me. I have been to over seventy-five countries and lived in six and to this day I still think the biggest culture shock I ever had was moving to North Carolina to go to college.

I had always wanted to go to North Carolina for school, and after getting the Park Scholarship to attend I was over the moon. I was sure it was going to be just like home but with more adventures and more diverse people. Bigger, and better!

I had not considered the stark differences between the Bible Belt and the swing state of Ohio. While I was raised in a town where social class dominated, Raleigh was a place where color mattered equally or more than social class. I thought racism so blatantly out in the open shouted almost with pride was merely something grandparents too senile to know better did, and that history books talked about. It turned out to be as out in the open as if there were no laws against it.

I hadn't imagined a pastor shouting at me on my way to class at 8 AM that I would be going to hell for wearing pants as a woman. My Ohioan liberal friends' outlook on sex was far more open at eighteen than the girls I roomed with, many of whom were still waiting for their first kiss. I felt like an alien in a place I had won a scholarship to attend.

It was complex and confusing for me to wrestle with the fact that my America from small-town Ohio was the same as the Confederate flag totting racist hunter in my Spanish class, who thought my place was in the kitchen.

How could we both be Americans? What did it mean

to be American? I was not an American for many North Carolinians but a Yankee, which they said with disdain. Did they know the Yankees had won the war? It was the Yankees that had all the higher educational institutions and most of the booming economy during the Civil War. I wondered if they had the same history books. Where do you turn to find America if it can be so blatantly different for so many people?

My quest to find America took me to Ghana, as far as I could get from what I knew, in order to explore what I didn't know about myself and what it meant to be "from the US."

There I found that everyone seemed to be looking for themselves in someone else. The African Americans thought they would feel at home in Africa, but most were considered as American as me to the Africans there. Instead of a sense of belonging friends told me they felt more out of place than they could have ever imagined.

I never thought I would 'blend' in Africa, so I started to learn to love being the outsider, and how being on the outside gives you the distance from others' judgments to truly understand you on the inside. If others see me as an outsider, their opinions can't be the same as mine because they don't see me as a part of them. Finally, I had space to look inside, and sort out who and what I wanted to be for myself. Perhaps my dad was able to do this for himself in America as he explored the English culture and way of life.

REFLECTIONS ON MY LIFE

I don't regret my decision to leave the Amish community. I could have stayed, been a troublemaker, and perhaps helped make some changes, but I chose a different path. Some of the people I knew who were rebellious at the time tend to be the more forward-thinking Amish today. They read more broadly than most Amish and realize that the rules and traditions are just that: rules and traditions. They stayed because they liked the positive aspects of the community. Some of them became community leaders, preachers, and deacons in the church with the ability to positively influence the culture.

I think most of them now believe that we receive forgiveness for our sins from Jesus, not by earning it through our works or by following rules. Most Christians don't believe forgiveness can be earned. When I was growing up, the Amish message focused on doing the best you could and hoping good works were enough to earn you a place in heaven. This ideology had already shifted by the time I went to my memm's funeral. There I heard a message similar to that of most Protestant churches—the belief that people are saved by grace, not by works.

Some people like my brother John stayed Amish because leaving the community means giving up so much of the culture of support and togetherness. I gave up a great deal—my family, my friends, and the sense of community.

I don't know my brothers and sisters, as well as most people know their siblings. We now enjoy each other's company, and I appreciate that the culture has changed enough that I can go home now and be greeted with a welcoming smile. However, I don't know them, in the same way, I would have if I had remained part of the community, growing old with them. It is very different than if I had known their children and they knew mine as they all grew up together.

Yet I believe I gained more than I lost. I made my own choices, thoughtfully and with consideration, and am pleased with how I have lived my life. I have gotten to do so many things I would never have had the opportunity to do. For these experiences, I am deeply grateful. God's grace showed me the path to help others and make a difference in the world. I have enjoyed every moment and every step of the way, through both the struggles and the happiest moments of my life.

In many ways, I feel fortunate to have grown up Amish. My father set a good example as a hardworking, honest man and instilled in me a strong work ethic. I owe much of my drive and persevering attitude to him, my family, and the Amish community in general.

Even my religious convictions and beliefs, although they have evolved through my journey, stemmed first from my time in the Amish community. While their rigid adherence to rules and doctrine may appear to stifle self-expression and growth, it nevertheless provides a solid foundation for strong faith, the importance of family and community, and compassion for others. The more flexible beliefs I now hold integrated into the earlier Amish teachings as I read the Bible from Genesis through Revelation. Over time my continuing biblical studies have shaped these beliefs into a strong faith in a God of grace, not of rules and regulations.

I am exceedingly thankful that my family is more accepting of me today. I feel certain that my brothers Eli and Jacob are happy with their lives and are grateful that my father intervened and talked them out of leaving the Amish community.

I believe that God had a different plan for me. Without His direction and guidance in my life, I could have never made it to where I am today. God placed key people in my path throughout my life to help and guide me through the difficult times.

Next to my love of family, raising four children and two stepchildren, I consider my greatest accomplishment to be my education and medical career. When I look back over the communications that led to my acceptance at the University of Cincinnati College of Medicine, I ask myself *Would I have accepted my application?*

In the current day and age, the answer would most likely be no. However, when I applied to medical school no computers, grammar checkers, or spellcheck existed. Instead, I used correction fluid to fix mistakes in my typed letters. My letters also clearly reflected the strong cultural difference between me and typical applicants. Medical school, although challenging, was not as hard as I had anticipated. It did require dedication and long hours of studying every day. During my years of medical school, residency, and early practice, I not only grew educationally but culturally as well.

My medical career has been amazingly rewarding, and a unique opportunity. After thirty years, I still enjoy practicing medicine. My favorite portion of my career has been emergency medicine. I relish the many challenges and the need for quick decision-making. Additionally, it incorporates my faith; in difficult moments, I always channel my thoughts: *Lord, guide my hands.*

If I could change or improve one part of my life, it would be to have spent more time with my children as they were growing up. I wish I had shared and taught them more of my spiritual beliefs. I am proud of my children and their accomplishments. We cannot get the past back, though, and I hope I can do better in the remaining years of my life.

My childhood, my culture, and the life I continue to live have shaped me in positive ways and brought me amazing gifts. I am thankful to have a wife and children I love, faith in Christ, a profession I adore, and the sense that I have worked to make the world a better place.

In life, it is not where you come from that matters, but what you do with the tools you have been given. The Amish culture and religion gave me the foundation I needed to reach my goals and get where I am today, and I could not be happier.

ACKNOWLEDGMENTS

I owe special thanks to many people but in particular Eli Hochstetler and John Schmidt. They were strong friends and advisers in my early Christian development. Ernie Hershberger was responsible for getting me started on the path to education and my eventual career. Mike and Kathy Sleutz and their extended family served as constant support and comfort.

Joan Miller, I can say without reservation, was the most important influence in my life. Not only did she provide me with the encouragement and motivation to stay in college, but she also helped me understand my parents and family better. She truly was a friend and counselor during a critical part of my life.

Numerous other professors also provided invaluable guidance and assistance at Kent State and helped me prepare for medical school. Dr. Don and Ann Nofziger served as kind family support throughout my medical school years and residency.

MJ, my ex-wife, was both a support and a difficult challenge in my life. She gave me four beautiful children: Elizabeth, Michael, Kristina, and Sara. I purposefully did not elaborate much on her part in my life, because it was difficult for me and all four of the children. If this story is to be told in more detail, I think they would be the best ones to do that. Divorce was obviously not something I ever thought would be a part of my life. Father John, a Catholic priest and a dear close friend provided strong support and guidance during my divorce.

My wife, Patricia, has been my strong companion and support as well as a role model for my four children. It is my hope that with her, my children got to see what a normal relationship should be.

So many other valuable and supportive people helped me through my life's journey to becoming a physician, I cannot possibly name all of them: professors at the University of Cincinnati College of Medicine, the colleagues and friends who helped me adapt to a new culture and a career, the many influential people both in my professional practice and in my religious and social life. I am exceedingly grateful for all these friends and advisers.

If you want to learn more about the Amish culture, ways of life, and my youth I encourage you to read the Appendix section.

A DAUGHTER'S AFTERWORD

Most of us face a moment in our lives when we are challenged to define ourselves.
Who am I?
Some people never bother to answer this question. When you are forced at a young age to make

difficult, life-altering choices, oftentimes you must define morals and values for yourself. Growing up we are all exposed to both good and bad, right and wrong, and all the grays in between. Each person has to determine their own path in life because nothing is either black or white. It takes strength of character to go out and create your own community, with or without your family. Establishing your morals in a world that allows so many excuses to ignore them is true courage. Life isn't about being perfect or even finding happiness here on Earth; it is about making the best of what you are given and working to improve the world around you.

My dad took up the challenge to define himself on his own terms, even with all the naysayers constantly telling him he was wrong. He became a doctor who has saved countless lives and helped thousands of people live healthier. He held strong to his values of community, hard work, perseverance, and doing what is right. And while his faith might have wavered as he looked for answers, he never gave up the search. He had the courage to clearly define himself, for himself, and to do so while keeping the greater good always in mind and helping others along the way.

When the time comes for you to define who you truly are and what you are made of, I hope you can do it as definitively as my father did. Your choices may not come without regrets, but I hope you are always aiming for the best possible result and sticking to your inner values, even if they differ at times from those around you.

To learn more about the Amish culture, ways of life, and my father's youth I encourage you to read the Appendix section.

APPENDIXES

GLOSSARY OF TERMS

Considering that Pennsylvania Dutch is not in and of itself a separate language, but rather a dialect of German, many of these words and expressions have no standard spelling. The language is almost entirely verbally transmitted; English and German are used for writing. Based on the phonetics of the pronunciation, I have done my best to write the words as I believe they would be spelled.

- *Albaht, ish da datt dehiem?* - Albert, is your dad at home?
- *Boova es ischt tzite fah uh schtay* - mBoys, it's time to get up.
- *Broota* - brother
- *Datt* - dad
- *de Grose Gehme* - communion
- *Dah Eli ischt dehehm* - Eli is home
- *Datt, vehr ischt sela mann?* - Dad, who is that man?
- *Duh varscht bessa op vahn duh gestaubasht vahn duh graunk vaust vie ein babee* - You would have been better off if you died when you were sick as a baby.
- *Es ischt tsoo fiel. Ich kahns ischt baud nicht mahha vahn sie mich finna vie dah Jonas es ischt deine schult* - It's too much. I can hardly manage it. If they find me like Jonas it is your fault.
- *Es ischt tzite fah uh schtay* - It's time to get up.
- *Giddy up* - go [for the horses]

- *Gmay* - church
- *Grossdatte* - grandfather
- *Grossmomme* - grandmother
- *Gute* - good
- *Guten tag* - good morning
- *Hooooo* - stop [for the horses]
- *"Ich bein ischt ahm ruhm gooka!"*- I'm just looking around!
- *Mahs ischt vie nix gehappened het* - Just act like nothing happened
- *Memm* - mom
- *Mit-taug essa* - lunch
- *Nevahuka* - best man and maid of honor
- *Onfung* - beginning
- *Ordnung (de adniks gehme)* - the church doctrine or rules
- *Sel iz ischt vie es ischt* - That is just the way it is.
- *Sel ischt dah Albaht. Her iz mya brutta ischt vie dah Sam dia brutta ischt* - Well, that is Albert. He's my brother, same as Sam is your brother.
- *Shvesta* - sister
- *Vas bischt du am duah?* - What are you doing?
- *Vehr ischt sela mann?* - Who is that man?
- *Vi bist du?* - How are you?
- *Xzit-nung* - witness
- *Yah, ich grek iehn fahdich* - Yes, I'll get him for you.

FAMILY TREE

Samuel M. Miller
March 14, 1920
Son of Mose S. and Rebecca (Mast) Miller
&
Esther Barkman
August 26, 1920
Daughter of Jacob and Lizziean (Beachy) Barkman

<u>Children</u>
Mose - February 12, 1947
Lizzie Ann - February 8, 1948
Eli - August 11, 1949
Jacob - February 2, 1951
Albert - May 15, 1953
Mary - June 22, 1954
Anna - December 30, 1955
Susie - May 13, 1956
Esther - Jan. 31, 1959
John - August 21, 1961
Ella - December 1, 1964

LETTERS

When I went through my old scrapbooks, memories came swarming back. Although not everything in my life was positive, for the purposes of this book I have tried to focus on the good aspects. After the newspaper article about my journey was published, I received numerous letters of support and encouragement. An old friend even wrote to congratulate me: "I remember a young boy telling me his dream was to go to medical school." That boy was me.

Some of my favorite letters are reprinted here.

U N I O N H O S P I T A L

659 BOULEVARD
HAROLD P. A
LOGAN L. DU

June 30, 1983

Albert S. Miller, M.D.
General Surgical Resident
Huron Road Hospital
13951 Terrace Road
~ ... 44112

MEDICAL SCHOOL LETTERS
OF REFERENCE

KENT STATE UNIVERSITY, TUSCARAWAS CAMPUS

August 15, 1978

Dear Sir:

I first met Bert when counseling incoming freshman students at the Tuscarawas Campus of Kent State University. After estimating his reading speed to be about 30 words per minute, I questioned him about his readiness to enter college. It was then that I learned that he never attended high school. I was both amazed at his enthusiasm, stamina, and sincerity and also concerned about his naivete and what seemed to me to be unrealistic goals (i.e., medical school). He insisted on carrying a full, heavy load and subsequently found that he had bitten off too much, and his grades reflected it.

In spite of setbacks, Bert learned how to adjust to academia. He supported himself by working at the local hospital while carrying a full load. His struggle against the odds was an inspiration to me as well as others who knew him. He never asked for exceptions but he often asked for help. He was enjoyable to invest time in as the rewards were so visible.

Bert took three psychology courses while he was here between 1974 and 1976. He did increasingly well in each subsequent course and became more interested in psychology. Bert was active in class and prompt in his assignments. He is above average in intelligence and extremely persistent.

I would predict that Bert would make an excellent family physician. His concern for people is genuine; his sensitivity is acute. Bert is very likable and his smile is contagious. He is decisive, mature, and hard-working.

I would highly recommend that Bert be given a chance to fulfill his "impossible dream."

Most sincerely,
Joan Miller
Psychology Department

ROBINSON MEMORIAL PORTAGE COUNTY HOSPITAL
RAVENNA, OHIO

January 16, 1979

Dear Sir:

It is with great pleasure that I write this letter
of recommendation for Mr. Albert Miller.

Bert, as his friends call him, has been an employee
of Robinson Memorial Hospital since June 13, 1977. He
was transferred to the Respiratory Care Department
on July 11, 1978, where he came under my direct
supervision and began his on-the-job training for
Respiratory Care.

During the workday, the pace of the department
may change several times, from routine therapy
procedures to life-saving situations, and the
individual responsible for accepting these changes
must be ready and able to cope with the situation
at hand.

Bert has been exceptionally versatile in these
situations and accepts them as part of his normal
duties.

He requires little or no supervision, but is
always open to constructive criticism, and learning
new skills.

He has no difficulty communicating with supervisory
personnel, his peers, and most importantly, the
patients with whom he comes in contact.

Bert also has no problems understanding both the
physical and emotional needs of the patient, but at
the same time maintains the professionalism required
to get the job done.

I have no doubt that Bert could successfully excel
in any profession of his choosing.

Respectfully,
Terry W. Stage, R.R.T.

Dear Mr. Miller,
One article in yester
Beacon magazine deepl
my heart.
You will be daily
prayers that you r
-tinue to be blessed
good fortune, cour
prosperity. May
keep your enthu
& of purpose
to

LETTERS OF SUPPORT

26 June 1978

Dear Bert:

Years ago when I worked at Union Hospital in Dover I knew of an Amishman's dream to attend college and hopefully someday become a doctor. In the course of day-to-day life, one encounters so many people who have dreams. Some of the dreams are more plausible than others, but the percentage of them that come to fruition is relatively low. Still, of all those people who have shared their dreams with me, Bert Miller's is one of those that stands out in my memory. Not because he was wilder or more improbable than others that I have encountered before or since, but because there was something special about this ex-Amish kid's dream. I have always wondered what happened to him.

Sunday morning I found out. My coffee grew cold and was forgotten as I read the article. I couldn't quite believe it so I read it again. Congratulations, Bert! You've done it so far and you're going to go all the way! As my friend Nancy, who is working on her doctorate said, "Right now he's come further than both of us put together." She's right, as usual. I don't think I would have had the courage to do half of what you have done already.

I am particularly happy that the story appeared when it did, as I am going to move to Harrisburg, Pennsylvania, in less than two weeks, so I just caught it in time. If you have a chance, I really would like to take you out to dinner before I leave Kent forever. If you like, give me a call at home (███████) or Monday through Friday between 8:00 am and 4:30 pm at the office (███████) and we can make arrangements.

If perchance I don't see you, congratulations again! It will still be tough, but the worst is over.

Sincerely,

Ted Wm Hanson

June 26th, 1978

Dear Mr. Miller,

The article in yesterday's Beacon magazine deeply touched my heart.

You will be daily in my prayers that you may continue to be blessed with good fortune, courage, and prosperity. May you always keep your enthusiasm and intent of purpose, and many you continue to receive the divine guidance that has led you to where you are today.

Let your hardships fortify your spirit and help you to become a better person. Perhaps your mission will one day be revealed to you by your parents' recognition.

No matter what - more power to you!

Please accept this gift as a small token of the appreciation I feel for your great courage, stamina, and efforts.

May God continue to bless you always.

Mrs. Linda Martin

KENT STATE UNIVERSITY

COLLEGE OF ARTS AND SCIENCES

June 28, 1978

Dear Mr. Miller:

It was with great interest that I read the feature article about you in the recent Beacon Journal. I hope you were pleased with the article since it appeared to me to be written sympathetically and to be well done.

I have enclosed a credit evaluation made for you in connection with your present senior status on the basis of your Psychology major and pre-medicine concentration. If you are attending during our summer sessions, more of that work could be included in the evaluation and there are certain other aspects of this estimate which could be changed depending on your selection of courses at several points. For example, the number of "upper-division" hours remaining (13) would be reduced appreciably if you were to select the 30000 level of Chemistry series mentioned under section IV.

If you have any questions concerning this information, please feel free to visit our office to speak to Miss Parsons who made the evaluation or to me or one of the other Deans. As you approach graduation, I would remind you that your application must be in our office during the first two weeks of the quarter preceding the one in which you expect to graduate.

Sincerely yours,

Janet M. Hoover
Associate Dean

Bert,

I was visiting friends in Akron on Sunday and saw the article about you in the Beacon. I was very interested in the article and also very impressed, you definitely have "guts."

My philosophy is that God does not saddle you with anything that you can't handle and that things work out the way they are supposed to, however, you still have to work for it. This philosophy has helped me through a lot of trying times. Things seem to be working out for you although I know it hasn't been easy.

Before I moved, I told Terry that I regretted not having gotten to know you, Terry, and Rhonda better. It seems as though people hurry about their business and never really get a chance to enjoy other people and share experiences. I am at fault too.

Just thought I'd write a note to you and tell you that I'll be thinking about you.

God be with you,

Sue Taft

THE AMISH

A BRIEF HISTORY

If you didn't grow up in the Midwest US or near an Amish community, you might not know much about the Amish, or only know what you've seen in reality TV shows or the movie Witness. The history of the Amish is a fascinating tale of a people who came to this continent in the early years of the United States to escape religious persecution.

The Amish church is an offshoot of the Mennonite church. Menno Simons, a former Catholic priest, broke away from the Catholic Church as part of the Protestant Reformation. Jacob Ammon was a Mennonite bishop who split from the Mennonites because he felt that people should live more separately from the rest of the world. He thought clothing should set members apart and that the Amish should not subscribe to modern inventions but live as close to the life and words of the Bible as possible. He believed that many modern inventions were worldly evils that would cause people to drift away from God.

From a small band of 6,000 in 1900 to an estimated 270,000 members today, Amish communities continue to grow and thrive. Today the Amish exist only on the North American continent; the last European congregation ceased in 1937. Attempts to expand beyond the United States and Canada have thus far been unsuccessful[3].

No official census of Amish communities has been taken,

[3] Kraybill, Donald B., et al. *The Amish*.

so the exact number of Amish is difficult to calculate. Many experts expected Amish communities to diminish in number and ultimately combine with other ethnicities and religions in the typical assimilation process of Americanization. Yet even as the stereotypical Amish of old are fading away, their communities have expanded in both population and territory while maintaining much of their unique identity[4]. Although more people are leaving the Amish church today than in the past, it is still an uncommon occurrence.

The Amish are a collection of independent congregational communities. They have much in common, although each church follows its own doctrine (*Ordnung*) or community practices, and its specific guiding principles and rules[5]. While many churches share similar rules and principles, others can be quite different. Regardless, they strive to maintain their ways and religious beliefs in the face of modern pressures.

RELIGIOUS PRACTICES

Historically, the Amish followed the strict doctrines of the church as the only way to find favor with God and earn their way to heaven. The Old Order Amish still firmly hold on to the stern and steadfast belief of my youth that if

[4] Kraybill, Donald B., et al. *The Amish.*
[5] Kraybill, Donald B., et al. *The Amish.*

you are born Amish you must remain Amish to go to heaven. Along with so many other traditions, however, some Amish faith is changing—from the traditional belief system to one where you are saved through grace. Consequently, I believe the shunning that I experienced has significantly lessened. It is my belief that the more the Amish read the Bible, the more accepting they become of others' beliefs.

According to my brother John, "Amish is a cultural way of life with rules that limit our exposure to modern equipment and technology, giving us quieter lifestyles. Religion is our belief in Jesus who died for all our sins, and by the grace of God, is the only way to heaven. We can't work our way into heaven, but if we believe in Jesus our Savior, He will guide us to do good things. As written in John chapter 3, verse 16: 'For God so loved the world that He gave His only begotten Son, that whosoever believeth in Him should not perish, but have everlasting life.'" KJV

The Amish are about community; everything the Amish do is for the good of the community. While individualism is praised, rewarded, and celebrated in America, the Amish discourage individuality and instead foster a belief in the strength of community. Neighbors help each other in the harvest, without being asked. Family, relatives, and church members show up to help with births, accidents, deaths, and whatever trials and tribulations occur throughout life. In an Amish community, it is rare to feel alone. Someone is always just around the corner to lend a helping hand, assist in paying for medical expenses, or participate in a circle of support.

Each Amish church consists of a community that is within an easy buggy drive and small enough to fit everyone inside a member's home, shed, or barn for Sunday worship services. That means that a church is typically limited to probably 10 to 25 families, depending on family size. During the winter, church services are held inside the house, and in the summer generally in a shed or barn.

My family hosted church services throughout the year because we had space both heated in winter and shaded in summer. On days we hosted, we got out of bed even earlier than usual to get everything ready. Usually, we set up the benches the night before, but we had to finish all the regular chores and prepare the food before people started to arrive.

The church consists of four preachers, including the bishop, who is the head of the church, and a deacon. My father, Samuel, was the deacon in our Old Order Amish church. Services are held every other Sunday, and the week in between is designated for visiting friends, family, neighbors, or a neighboring church.

Church services usually begin at 8:00 am, with people starting to arrive by 7:30, and last for three to four hours. Services open with singing, though no musical instruments are allowed in the church or even in the home, except for the harmonica.

Next, the preachers go to a separate room to discuss among themselves what the sermons will be about and who will deliver them. When they come back in, the singing stops. Each service has two sermons, delivered by two different preachers. The first sermon is usually a shorter sermon known as the *Onfung*, the beginning, and lasts about thirty minutes. After the first sermon, there is a prayer. Then the deacon reads a portion of the scripture, followed by another prayer. After the second prayer the lead preacher at the service, either the bishop or another preacher, gives the main sermon, which may last an hour or more.

The speakers do not use notes, preaching only from their thoughts and memories. When the last preacher is finished speaking, he asks the other members on the bench (usually the four ordained members: bishop, deacon, and two preachers) and any other visiting preachers to give xzitnung, or to witness—essentially asking if they find any fault with his sermon. Each says in their own way, "The sermon was from the Word of God." The service closes with a final prayer and hymn.

Since the service is so long, lunch is served at the end. Church members visit and exchange news while children play tag or other simple games. People usually trickle home by midafternoon.

In addition to regular church services, the Amish hold big celebrations for certain religious holidays. Christmas and Easter are always celebrated, as well as Good Friday and Ascension Day. If the holiday falls on a Sunday, then that week's service is tailored to the occasion, but the church doesn't hold any specific holiday services.

The Amish don't consider December 25 the official date of Jesus' birth. They celebrate "Old Christmas" on January 6.

This does not include a gift exchange, a tree, or lights. Gifts are not the focus of Christmas, although exchanges of baked goods are common. Sometimes children receive a game, but food, cookies, and candies are always brought to share when people visit during the holiday season.

If the church has any business to handle, the service might go on even longer. Business matters to discuss and vote on include giving money for disaster relief or paying for a member's medical bills. Nonmembers and children cannot participate in or vote on community issues and are asked to leave the meeting.

On rare occasions, meetings deal with members who fail to follow the rules or to decide on punishment. Members who disobey the rules are present to hear their punishment but cannot vote. Members can also attend the meeting to repent and ask for forgiveness to prevent shunning.

The bishop is in charge of the church hierarchy and has the final say on matters. The deacon handles disciplinary enforcement. I believe that because my father was the deacon in our church, he and other family members treated me so harshly as a warning to other Amish who thought about leaving, especially my nieces and nephews. Community, values, and ties to God are what keep most questioning rebels in the Amish fold. I was an exception.

Misbehavior takes many forms in the Amish church. Members who disregard the rules are put beside the church (excommunicated). One member of our community had a guitar while he was a teenager and refused to give it up when he joined the church. He was allowed to attend services but couldn't take communion until he made things right.

Making things right with the church means asking forgiveness in front of the entire community, repenting, and correcting the error.

Members join the Amish church by choosing to be baptized, a decision usually made when youth are eighteen to twenty-two years old. Prior to joining they participate in six months of hour-long classes with the community's religious leaders at every Sunday service. I left the Amish community when I was eighteen and never joined the church. Those who don't join can't be a part of community decisions, take communion, or get married. Love and the thought of marriage are often what trigger youth to join.

Marrying between the different sects or church orders does occur, but a married couple never attends two different Amish churches; the couple chooses one of the churches to join. Moving from Old Order Amish to New Order Amish due to marriage is rare, but does happen, and switching orders isn't considered a sin.

Amish leadership positions are held for life. All married men in the district are eligible to fill the post of deacon and preacher, although in truth most of them don't want the responsibility.

After community-wide discussions to narrow down the list of candidates, all church members vote on who they think should be the leader. When the votes are tallied, usually about six men garner a minimum of two votes each to be in the running.

Elections are held through a lottery system. With all the candidates in a separate room, a set of Bibles, one for each candidate, is laid out. Inside one of the Bibles is a message: "You have been chosen to be a preacher (or deacon) by God." The Bibles are shuffled so no one knows which one contains the message.

Each candidate selects a Bible. Once the candidates have a Bible, they open it to reveal which member has the one with the message. The new leader is taken under the wing of the other preachers and educated for his position.

The church uses a similar lottery system to select a new bishop from the three current preachers. Sometimes preachers are selected quite young when they are first married and have just joined the church. My nephew, Joseph, was chosen as a preacher while still in his twenties. My family includes several other preachers as well—my brother, Jacob, my brother-in-law, Delbert, and my brother-in-law, Andy.

Because Amish preachers are drawn from the entire community population, some of them may have had a car during their Rumspringa days. They don't view the car itself as evil, but rather what it can be used for and its potential to erode the traditional Amish values. Being Amish means preserving the close ties to community, family, and faith. The strict rules are designed to maintain and uphold a lifestyle that they believe fosters closeness with God. Deacons in particular seek to protect these values by not allowing sins such as individualism or pride to deteriorate the Amish faith and lifestyle.

The Amish culture and belief system are based on doing the best we can on Earth, following the church rules, and living a life pleasing to God, in order to be able to spend eternal life with God and God's people in heaven. I think most Amish believe that good non-Amish people also go to heaven. They believe that people are held accountable for what they know, so those outside the Amish culture are not expected to follow church doctrine. However, those who are raised Amish and know "the way" must follow it.

Like all cultures around the world, the Amish aren't without their faults. What I find ironic is that in their quest to separate themselves from the material world by keeping life simple, they have in some way become more materialistic. Arguments erupt over the number of buttons allowed on a shirt or folds in a bonnet. Such trivial things become major conflicts that can split a district into distinct churches. They may even cause rifts in the very foundations, such as the division that separated the New Order Amish from the Old Order. Our original church district has been divided into different church districts several times.

CULTURAL PRACTICES

Most Amish turn their face to avoid being photographed, which they believe glorifies or draws attention to the individual. Such self-gratification is frowned on. Amish always seek to uphold the values of the Bible and not commit the deadly sin of pride. Marketing or advertising their goods with personal photographs is considered a form of vanity. While my siblings and I were growing up, we never had pictures taken of us. Today some parents in the younger generation of Amish now have photos of their kids.

One of the classic toys of the Amish are the famous faceless dolls. These dolls help prevent envy, another deadly sin and allow children to grow up to be their own individuals without imposing external ideals of beauty on them. Keeping the focus off of personal appearance helps promote community throughout a culture that emphasizes internal values over external beauty.

Farming has traditionally been the primary economic driver of Amish communities. When my parents first moved to Coshocton County, we were surrounded by English people, but the Amish have since bought up most of that land. My datt bought two additional farms adjacent to his land as they became available. My brother, Mose, lives on one of these farms down the road, near the sawmill that he started, and has done quite well with his lumber business. Brother Jacob lives on another farm my datt bought as the English moved out. He also started his own business, which includes a neighborhood hardware store and a shop where he builds items from metal such as carts, furniture, and related items.

Since the Amish tend to have many children, with six or more not uncommon, the population as a whole tends to grow quickly. Rapid growth means that there is not enough land for people to survive solely on farming. To compensate, many Amish have started to work in other areas, from lumber mills and construction to restaurants and sales. Due to the growth of the Amish community, this area has since been divided several times and added new church districts. My family's home farmstead is now in the Millcreek Church District. The geographical region of Holmes County and the surrounding counties now have the largest number of Old Order Amish church communities in the United States.

CHANGES

While the Amish resist change, they do adapt with the times. Church rules and customs change over time, making the Amish community a living and adapting body.

In order to compete in an ever more technological market, the Amish have had to comply with regulations on milking, baling, and livestock. Other changes, like those in farming equipment, have come about due to the inaccessibility of the older equipment. The Amish are not allowed to own modern equipment but can hire someone else to harvest for them. Some Amish still use traditional tools and equipment, many of which are now obsolete. Other families have simply decreased their crop farming or relied on English neighbors with a combine to harvest their fields.

When I was growing up, our church didn't allow bicycles, though they do now. I did have a cousin who had one since his church allowed them. I snuck over to learn to ride with him but never told my parents. I wrecked it once and just kept my scraped elbow covered until it healed.

Amish homes are a technology-free zone, reserving time for the family to spend with each other and in shared communion with God. For emergencies, some Amish had a payphone in a box in the barn or outside the home. Now those have mostly been replaced by cell phones, which are only turned on for use in extreme emergencies like a fire or health issues. For Amish who need cell phones or computers at work, most churches allow members to use them on the job, but not at home.

RECOLLECTIONS OF AN AMISH LIFE

A lot has changed since I was young. Many modern conveniences that most Americans take for granted simply didn't exist among the Amish of my youth. It wasn't that we were poor, but the rules of our church and community denied us many conveniences of modern life.

We didn't have indoor plumbing—no toilet, no bathtub, no running water in the house. Water came from a pump in the yard. When I needed to go to the bathroom I went to the outhouse—in the rain, snow, or cold winter night. Our outhouse was a rustic wooden structure the size of a small closet that covered a ditch in the ground. The hold never got cleaned out, but a drainage track allowed the contents to drain into the nearest stream or pond. That's not sanitary or even legal anymore.

Peeing wasn't a problem for me; I could do that just about anywhere. However, the outhouse was riddled with obstacles. Having to put on shoes in the dead of winter in -15°F, or shining a flashlight into a spider's gleaming eyes on hot summer nights, meant that I learned to not drink much water before bed.

Baths consisted of a big galvanized steel tub filled with water in the living room near the wood-burning stove, with water heated on the stove added to keep it warm during the winter months. Each member of the family took a turn in the basin.

Showers, when the weather got warm enough, were in the same place where Memm hung the laundry to dry and we slaughtered the pigs. A simple bucket with holes in the bottom sufficed.

Once or twice a week in the summer the iceman delivered giant blocks of ice for our non-electric refrigerator. The upper portion held the ice, and on lower shelves, we stored food, similar to a regular refrigerator. In between the ice and the shelves was a tray to catch the water as the ice melted. Sometimes we convinced Memm and Datt to buy an extra block of ice so we could make ice cream in our hand-cranked ice cream maker.

In the winter ice cream was even easier to make with ice from icicles, the pond, or the creek. When ice and snow were abundant, we collected it and put it either on the north side of the barn out of the sun or buried it under the straw in the hayloft to make it last longer.

By the time I was a teenager, our house had running water and indoor plumbing. My dad was very handy and was one of the first to install a bathtub and an indoor toilet with running water once they were allowed by the Gmay. Compared to going outside in the freezing cold to pump water in the winter, having warm water arrive with the turn of a tap was such a luxury!

The Amish live a very simple life. They rarely take vacations or go out to dinner. They certainly don't go to movies or do anything that would be considered worldly. Although I wasn't aware of it as a child, my parents occasionally went to an Amish vacation spot, a small community called Pinecraft in Sarasota County, Florida.

Pinecraft has a community center with games and activities where the Amish can gather to relax and have fun—play shuffleboard, sing, or attend church services. Although the houses have electricity, the neighborhood includes amenities typical of any Amish community, including Amish-oriented stores and Amish home cooking-style restaurants.

The Amish do not permit flying in airplanes, so taking such a vacation requires car or bus transportation. A transportation system known as the Amish bus travels at least two days a week, taking Amish passengers from Pennsylvania through Ohio to Florida. Some Amish go to visit family and friends, and in the winter they often go to Pinecraft simply for a vacation. Just like their English neighbors, the Amish like to get away from the cold from time to time.

My parents, like parents the world over, likely needed a break from their eleven children.

When I was seven or eight years old, my parents went on vacation without us kids. My oldest brother, Mose, wasn't old enough to watch us all, so our neighbors John Eiker and his wife, Esther, stayed at our place as temporary parents. They took care of us and made sure we got all the chores done.

While my parents were gone, a blizzard struck. The dirt road that led to our farm was buried in snowdrifts. The milkman couldn't get to the milk, and if he couldn't pick it up, it would spoil and we would lose it. Mr. Eiker came up with the brilliant idea to put the milk cans on our sleigh. I was too small to help, but my brothers had fun loading the milk cans on the sleigh and hitching up the team of horses. I watched from the house as they struggled up the road through the snow to the main road to wait for the milkman. We all felt quite proud of our ingenuity. Plus the hard work paid off—when Datt returned he was impressed with our innovative thinking.

DAYS ON THE FARM

The plan for the day was announced at breakfast. Sometimes someone had to go to town to pick up supplies, or Datt would go to the auction to buy or sell livestock.

Rainy days, when we had to stay indoors, we spent repairing broken equipment, cleaning out stalls, hauling manure, or mending harnesses. When the weather was good, we went straight from the breakfast table to hitch up the horses and get started on the planting, harvesting, or whatever seasonal farming task was at hand.

Spring was planting season. We needed to plow the field to form rows to plant the seeds. Early in the season, we had to cultivate the corn, keep the weeds out, and make sure the new seeds had space to grow. Weeds would grow between the rows, especially when the corn was little. To prevent these weeds from choking out the emerging corn, we used a cultivator, which has small spades that dig up the weeds between the rows of corn. Cultivating was a recurring task until the corn got big enough that the equipment no longer fit between the rows. By then the corn leaves created enough shade that the weeds couldn't grow between the rows.

While the corn was still short, the cultivator would throw dirt onto the young plants, covering them up. One of my jobs as a small boy was to follow behind my datt or older brother as they maneuvered the cultivator between the rows. I had to watch for any small plant that got buried and uncover it. Seeds had to be planted so they were covered enough to get the nutrition they needed and not be washed away by the rain, but not so deep that they couldn't find their way out of the soil into the sun.

Fall was harvest time. Harvest and planting occur in rotation—the hayfields one year become cornfields next year, and the next year either oats or wheat and then back to hay. This crop rotation is repeated over and over again.

The terms *straw* and *hay* are often used interchangeably by those who are unfamiliar with farming, but they are different. Straw is merely the stem of the grain once the edible parts are removed. It's used for bedding and to keep the stalls and sheds clean. Hay has nutritional value and serves as food for much of the livestock from different plants like timothy, clover, or alfalfa. The hay is cut very green and then dried in the sun.

Regardless of the crop, harvest was always the busiest time of year. We were racing against nature itself. Wheat and oats were ready to harvest once they grew into a tall, golden-yellow plant. We used an old-fashioned McCormick binder that cut the grain at its base and collected it into sheaves or bundles. As my datt cut the grain, we boys followed behind, making shocks out of these bundles. The shocks gave the grain more time to dry in the fields before being stored for the winter.

After a few days to a week, the shocks would be ready for the threshing machine. In our neighborhood, a group of four or five families teamed up to help each other with this task. My datt owned the thresher, which is a large, heavy piece of equipment designed to separate the grain from the straw as the sheaves are fed through. The machine was pulled by a tractor from field to field to accomplish the harvest at each family's home. The thresher would be parked in its position and the tractor used as the engine, hooked up to the motor by a pulley and a large belt.

On threshing day men used three or four wagons to haul the sheaves of grain from the field to the barn to be fed through the machine. The thresher separated the grain from the stalks, spewing the grain out the side into bags or a grain bin. The straw blew out the back of the thresher into the barn den.

Since my datt owned the thresher and was in charge of operating it at each farm in our group, I got to be part of the threshing team before I was actually old enough to handle any heavy work. Somebody needed to operate the blower to distribute the straw coming out the back into the barn. I wore a handkerchief over my nose and mouth to keep from inhaling the dust. When we took our lunch break, I was so dusty that someone had to brush me off with a broom before I could wash my hands to eat lunch. Despite the mess, I took pride in being part of such important work.

During the spring planting and growing season, rain is a highly valued commodity, but in the fall it can ruin a crop. At harvest time we needed at least two or three days with no rain so the hay had time to dry. After those two to three days, depending on how hot the sun was, we raked the hay into neat rows that could be gathered up to be moved into the barn. Because mechanized hay balers were not permitted, we loaded the loose hay onto a wagon with a hay loader, then stacked it in the hayloft above the cows and other animals for winter storage.

Putting the hay up was the hardest work. The hay was brought into the barn loose, collected on large hooks that pulled it off the wagon in a bundle. Hitched to a rope, pulley, and tackle, a horse-pulled the rope carrying the bundle up to the roof of the barn onto a track that led down into the barn den where the hook was released and dropped the hay into a pile. We had to distribute the hay by hand, filling the den evenly to allow storage of as much hay as possible. It was extremely hot work, especially when the den filled up and we were up against the roof of the barn.

Once the hay harvest was finished, we moved on to the corn. There are two ways to harvest corn: shucking by hand or with a corn picker. During my youth, nearly all the corn was harvested by hand shucking. With a team of horses hitched to a wagon, everyone who was available—usually three or four people per wagon—went out to husk.

The horses were well-trained in voice commands and rarely even needed a driver. *Giddy up* meant go and *hoooo* meant stop. We walked alongside the wagons as the horses pulled, removing each ear of corn from its stalk. My datt was always farthest from the wagon; he could do two rows in the time it took us to do one. When the wagon was full we unloaded it into the barn, then headed back out, repeating until the field was cleared.

Sometimes we used a corn picker, but we stopped using it when I was about twelve because it only created extra work. The only thing we gained with the automated picker was preserving the corn stalk, which wasn't all that useful. Instead, we used the corn picker to gather the green corn into sheaves that were later ground into silage to feed the cows. A full silo at the end of the harvest holds enough silage to last the whole year.

In the winter the cows were kept inside, both to protect them from the cold and because there was no grass for them to eat. The hay and straw were their food and bedding. We even saved the manure for fertilizer, spreading it over both pasture and fields before plowing and planting to infuse the soil with valuable nutrients.

Winter days were spent grinding up a feed for the pigs, chickens, and cows. The primary focus on our farm was dairy farming, so the cows ate most of the feed. During bad weather we mended farm equipment; we could do little in a field covered in snow.

Each day at around 11:30 AM we stopped work for lunch, regardless of the season. Before we went in for our lunch, we put all the horses back in their stalls in the barn for a rest and some feed. Lunch, our *mit-taug essa*, was the largest and heaviest meal of the day. Usually, Memm served whatever meat we had slaughtered recently, potatoes, and some noodles or vegetables. Memm had *mit-taug essa* ready when we came in from the fields so we all sat down to eat together.

If my memm and sisters had gone somewhere—quilting at a relative's house, or to visit friends—*mit-taug essa* was not prepared and lunch was a bit lighter. Before the women left they would have made sandwiches and something easy for us to heat up, like noodles, to eat in their absence. We would come in from the field, heat up anything left on the stove, eat quickly, clean up the kitchen, and head back out to the fields.

After mit-taug essa we hitched the horses up again and headed back to work until 4:30 or 5:00 PM. Supper was eaten before the evening chores and was usually lighter than lunch, and the fare varied according to season. In the summer we got cold milk banana soup, in the winter a hot soup, with some meat. When the ears of corn were ripe and ready, we would eat corn on the cob in place of the soup. Some days we each ate five or six ears of corn in a sitting. We always had dessert—a pie, a cake, something sweet. When I lived and worked on the farm, I ate a lot and was still quite skinny.

On the long summer evenings, we often hitched the horses up again after supper to get in a little more work in the fields before darkness set in. When I came in from the fields I went straight to bed; I was exhausted. Occasionally I grabbed a snack first, but summer basically meant I was working all the time that I wasn't asleep.

During the winter we sometimes read or ate some popcorn after supper. Reading the Bible wasn't encouraged; the church emphasized listening to the word of God in church and following the rules of the *Gmay*. Instead, we read one of several Amish newspapers: *The Budget*, *The Ohio Farmer*, or the quarterly *Farmer's Almanac*.

We had a few games like *Monopoly*, but those took time and we were always tired, so we didn't play them often. Card games that had decks without faces were allowed, such *Uno* or *Phase 10*. Face cards could stir up one of the seven deadly sins, vanity. So dolls and other play objects in my youth did not have faces, to help us avoid jealousy, Occasionally we played checkers or Chinese checkers as the winter evening shifted the day into night.

The weekends were somewhat less intense. Saturdays we cleaned and prepped everything to look its best for Sunday, including washing our buggies. On Sundays, we only did essential chores like milking the cows and feeding the animals. The rest of the day was spent at church or socializing.

After Jacob got married and left our house, I was the only one left at home to help my datt. It was a lot of work because Datt owned three farms, and my younger brother wasn't old enough to do much yet. On our home farm, we had dairy cows. On one we raised beef cattle. On one we kept miscellaneous livestock that needed less care. All three properties required tending the crops. The cattle and dairy farms both had large, lush pastures for grazing the animals. The beef farm also required bedding and feeding chores once a day. The biggest chore was milking the dairy cows at least twice a day.

That was the typical day-to-day Amish life of my youth.

ABOUT THE AUTHORS

ALBERT MILLER MD
AUTHOR & DOCTOR

Albert Miller was born and raised on an Amish farm. He never attended high school, having only completed his elementary school in an Amish parochial school which ended in eighth grade. After taking the GED test, he attended Kent State University, graduating in 1979. He was accepted into the University of Cincinnati College of Medicine, where he received a Doctorate of Medicine in 1983. He was board certified in Family Practice and had a private practice in Ohio. Dr. Miller has always practiced emergency medicine along with his family practice, and gradually transitioned to full-time emergency medicine. Holding a medical license in the states of Ohio, Virginia, Tennessee, Florida, and Alabama, he has served on an emergency medicine travel team that took him to the forementioned states. He has held Emergency Medical director positions at Mercy Hospital in Willard, Ohio, and Dale Medical Center in Ozark, Alabama. Currently, Dr. Miller works full-time as a staff emergency medicine physician at Flowers Hospital in Dothan, Alabama, and part-time at Dale Medical Center in Ozark, Alabama. Dr. Miller has always maintained a strong spiritual faith and he and his wife, Pat, are active members at Covenant United Methodist in Dothan, Alabama. Together they have served as team leaders on numerous medical missions serving the Ngobe Indian tribe in the country of Panama.

LIZ MILLER
AUTHOR, CONTENT CREATOR & EDUCATOR

L iz Miller has been a content creator and educator for 15 years across 5 countries and has traveled to over 75+ countries. She has loved storytelling from childhood and taught high school literature in addition to creating content for companies and developing curricula. Currently, she is the Communication Manager for GetSetUp, an online community and educational platform for older adults. She is dedicated to enhancing client communication through coaching, editing, and content creation. In addition to writing articles, books, and other content she has started her own line of bilingual children's stories.

Liz Miller earned her bachelor's degree in Visual and Verbal Communication, with concentrations in Psychology, Applied Arts, and Spanish at North Carolina State University. She also has a Master's Degree in Education with a focus on Digital Technology and has taken various marketing courses. In addition to writing articles and content, she has also started her own bilingual children's series of original stories including Dandelion Wishes, which is written in both English and Portuguese.

GRAZIELLE PORTELLA
ILLUSTRATOR, COVER & DESIGN

Grazielle Portella (b. 1989, Brazil) is a visual artist, designer, and researcher. She is currently a PhD student at the Fine Arts Faculty of the University of Lisbon (funded by the Foundation of Science and Technology - FCT). She holds a Master's in Digital Design (PUC-SP, 2016) and Bachelor's in Visual Design (UFRGS, 2012). Informed by philosophy, neuroscience, and aesthetics, she develops the concept of Slow Drawing, investigating contemplative, ethical, and effective practices in contemporary art. Has been selected at residencies such as L'AiR Arts Paris and Joya: AIR arte + ecología and exhibited her work in Lisbon, Barcelona, and Paris. Previously worked for Google (São Paulo, 2011-2017), Flaner (Paris/Lisbon), K Solutions (Paris), Actar Publishers, and Fundació Joan Miró (Barcelona).

Made in the USA
Columbia, SC
02 August 2022

64484816R00186